small group

Living
under God's protection

The armour of God

Florence MacKenzie

Scripture Union, 207–209 Queensway, Bletchley, MK2 2EB, England.
email: info@scriptureunion.org.uk
web site: www.scriptureunion.org.uk

We are an international Christian charity working with churches in more than 130 countries providing resources to bring the good news about Jesus Christ to children, young people and families – and to encourage them to develop spiritually through the Bible and prayer.

As well as our network of volunteers, staff and associates who run holidays, church-based events and school Christian groups, we produce a wide range of publications and support those who use our resources through training programmes.

©Florence MacKenzie, 2002
First published 2002
ISBN 1 85999 450 4

British Library Cataloguing-in-Publication Data

A catalogue record for this book is available from the British Library.

Cover design: Carsten Lorenz

Printed in Great Britain by Ebenezer Baylis & Sons Ltd, The Trinity Press, Worcester and London.

Contents

*This Bible study is dedicated
to the memory of my mother,
whose Christian testimony influenced
me throughout my childhood and later years.
I acknowledge with thankfulness the
firm grounding in scriptural principles
which I received from her.*

Introduction

When I first considered writing a Bible study on the armour of God, I expected difficulty owing to the nature of the subject matter. I knew that our enemy, Satan, would be opposed to any writing that exposed him as a real, malevolent being who has already been defeated by Jesus' death and resurrection. Anticipating this, I sought the assistance of trusted Christian friends and told them that I would write the study only if they committed to pray for me throughout the writing process. They assured me that they would pray and I am grateful to God and to them for this support. I believe that the Lord truly bound Satan through the course of writing this study – never underestimate the very real power of prayer.

I believe it was necessary to write this study for several reasons. Firstly, I needed to become more familiar with what Ephesians 6:10–18 actually teaches. Feeling a personal need to study and apply biblical truths regarding a certain passage or topic is always a major reason for me writing. Secondly, I think that Christians are often ignorant of the fact that we do have an enemy and we are engaged in warfare with him. Too often believers attribute spiritual failures in their lives to, for example, a weakness in their personalities or to difficult circumstances, and they fail to grasp that, on many occasions, they are being attacked by Satanic powers. Thirdly, I believe that this passage has much to tell us about who we are in Christ – 'Be strong in the Lord' – it's because of our identity as people in whom the Holy Spirit lives that we can be confident in this battle. We must never think that we, in our own strength, are a match for Satan.

My desire for you is that, as you complete this study, you will see the incredible resources which the Lord has put at the disposal of every Christian believer. The armour is not for those who think they are already strong nor, conversely, for those who see themselves as being particularly weak – it is for all who are on the Lord's side and are concerned about retaining the victory which he has already won. May he strengthen and encourage each of you as you study and apply his Word to your everyday lives.

How to use this study

Welcome to the *Living under God's protection* Bible study. My desire is that as you study and share your findings with others, you will be drawn into a closer relationship with the Lord and will be better equipped to be a winner in your spiritual warfare.

This Bible study has two main emphases: the first is to encourage you to dig deep into the word of God because this is our main guide for living, and the second is to help you apply this word to your daily life. Only God's word is completely trustworthy and, if we are going to live in a way which will honour and please him, then we need to know what he says in the Bible. This is the touchstone of all debate. However, being merely familiar with what the Bible says is, in itself, insufficient. In order for God's word to be real and vital, there needs to be application of the truths that we read about there. The best way to do this is to co-operate with the Holy Spirit. Ask him to help you take on board what God is saying to you in the Bible. Ask him to apply his word to you so that there is no way that you can remain unchanged by its power. Biblical truth applied to our lives by the Holy Spirit results in spiritual growth and changed attitudes and behaviour.

This study is for either individual or group application. If you are sharing your answers with others in a group, this is a good way to support and encourage one another. However, the most important part of the study is in preparation. Allow yourself plenty of time to read the questions and the Bible references. Get alone with the Lord and his word. Ask him for his help as you go through each of the questions. Don't concern yourself about 'wrong answers' – do as much as you can, as completely as you can. This is really your learning period. Fully prepared in this way, you will find that you will receive immense benefit from the subsequent sharing in your group. You will also be in a much stronger position to contribute thoughtfully and meaningfully – this will be greatly appreciated by both your leader and other group members.

The time taken in preparation will vary from person to person. Don't be concerned if it takes a while to complete each chapter. My intention is that the questions and Bible verses will cause you to linger in the Lord's presence. However, I suggest you avoid the temptation of answering all the questions from a chapter in one sitting, the day or evening before you meet with the rest of your group to share what you have written. It might overwhelm you to tackle a whole chapter at a time. Instead, you will probably find it helpful to divide up each chapter into study sections. For example, each one is already divided into three parts. Depending on the frequency with which your group meets, you might wish to do each section over two days, giving a six day preparation time, with about twenty minutes per day devoted to answering the questions, reading the Bible verses and praying about the application to your own life. This could be a suitable pattern if your group meets every week. On the other hand, if you meet with others every two weeks, you could complete the study by spending around twenty minutes every other day, or by spending less time each day but preparing your answers over a ten or twelve day period. The way you prepare is essentially up to you – different people have different needs and responsibilities – but the important thing is that you develop a pattern of study which works for you and then stick to it! If you haven't approached Bible study in this way before, you will find the discipline involved to be extremely beneficial in your walk with the Lord.

May each of you face each day 'dressed for victory' as you put on the armour of God, remembering always, in the words of seventeenth century preacher William Gurnall, to *take special care not to trust in the armour of God, but in the God of the armour.*

Notes for leaders

Leading a Bible study is a great privilege and responsibility. Not only do leaders need to thoroughly prepare the study material, but they also need to prepare themselves. This involves being in a close relationship with the Lord, arising out of personal Bible study and prayer, along with a commitment to live their lives to God's glory. No matter how much natural talent leaders might have, they are absolutely dependent upon the Lord for wisdom and help in leading their groups. My desire is that, as you study this material together with your group members, you will draw your strength from him and will become more like him.

Encourage your group members to write down their answers to the questions before coming to the Bible study meeting. In my own experience as group leader, and in talking with other leaders, I've found this to be a vital part of Christian growth. Preparation allows an opportunity to be guided by the Holy Spirit in answering the questions, whereas an 'off-the-cuff' response during the meeting, with no prayerful preparation time, is less likely to be helpful to others in the group. Asking that all members of your group prepare each chapter in advance of your meeting helps to encourage timid, less knowledgeable members to contribute their responses on a more equal footing with spiritually mature members – this, in turn, can lead to greater spiritual growth and unity within the group.

This Bible study will take about sixty to ninety minutes to discuss people's answers to the questions. It's important that all questions are covered in your meeting, because if you get into the habit of not discussing the final questions in each chapter, your members might not prepare answers to these questions for future chapters. I suggest, therefore, that you prepare a time schedule in advance of your meeting – write down your start time at the beginning, then the time you expect to complete the first section, and the second section, and finally the third section of the chapter to be discussed. In this way, you should be able to keep track of your time and know whether you need to slow down or speed up in discussing your group's responses.

May the Lord be constantly at your side as you seek to lead others into a deeper knowledge of him.

1| Armour – who needs it?

'Finally, be strong in the Lord and in his mighty power. Put on the full armour of God so that you can take your stand against the devil's schemes. For our struggle is not against flesh and blood, but against the rulers, against the authorities, against the powers of this dark world and against the spiritual forces of evil in the heavenly realms. Therefore put on the full armour of God, so that when the day of evil comes, you may be able to stand your ground, and after you have done everything, to stand. Stand firm then, with the belt of truth buckled around your waist, with the breastplate of righteousness in place, and with your feet fitted with the readiness that comes from the gospel of peace. In addition to all this, take up the shield of faith, with which you can extinguish all the flaming arrows of the evil one. Take the helmet of salvation and the sword of the Spirit, which is the word of God. And pray in the Spirit on all occasions with all kinds of prayers and requests. With this in mind, be alert and always keep on praying for all the saints.'
Ephesians 6:10–18 (NIV)

Ephesians 6:10–18 is the classic passage in Scripture on the believer's armour. It has it all. Other passages shed light on the subject, but none comes close to this 'mother lode' of spiritual gold. And because this portion of the Bible is so familiar, we can easily write it off with a yawn, thinking 'been there, read that'. And, of course, nothing would please the enemy more.
Rich Miller [1]

When was the last time you were in a fight? Last week? Last year? Several years back in primary school? If you're a Christian, then you've been fighting much more recently than that. Would you believe me if I told you that you're actually in a fight right now? The fight you're engaged in is part of the all-out warfare between Christians and their enemy, Satan. In fact, our enemy is so dangerous that God has provided special protection or armour for us to wear, which we're told about in Paul's letter to the Ephesians.

This letter was written to the church in Ephesus around AD 60 during Paul's imprisonment in Rome. Historically it has been recognised as having universal significance for the church, however, as its message is relevant for all Christians, whatever their time and place in history – and that includes us in the twenty-first century.

One of the main themes of the book of Ephesians concerns the spiritual blessings which believers have in the Lord Jesus Christ. In order to set the armour passage (Ephesians 6:10–18) in context, we need to start by considering these benefits. Next, we will take a look at why it is necessary for the Christian to be kitted out in the full armour of God and, finally, we will consider the importance of various commands which are given in this passage.

The Christian's spiritual inheritance

The privilege of partaking in the riches of Christ's grace and glory as part of His Body is not without its responsibilities. We should not expect to sit and walk with Him unless we are also willing to stand for Him in the battle against Satan. He has already won the war for us – it's our responsibility to hold on to His victory.
Warren W Wiersbe 2

The book of Ephesians has been described as detailing the Christian's wealth (chapters 1–3); the Christian's walk (chapters 4 and 5, through to 6:9); and the Christian's warfare (6:10 to the end). The first of these, the Christian's wealth, refers to the spiritual blessings which believers receive from the Lord when they trust in him.

Read Ephesians 1:3–14

Q List the benefits which are given to those who are in Christ.

Q Write out Ephesians 1:3 and 1:20 in your own words.

Q Notice that a phrase which occurs in each of these verses is 'in the heavenly realms' (see also Ephesians 2:6 and Ephesians 6:12). What do you understand by this and how is it linked to the Christian's spiritual warfare? (See again Ephesians 6:12.)

Why do we need the full armour of God?

We are engaged in warfare

We are never to forget that we are individual units in a great army. We are not fighting some personal, private war. This is not the position at all. We are simply individual soldiers in a great army which is fighting a great campaign. In other words, the real, the ultimate issue is not so much my fight with the devil, as God's fight with the devil. This is the way to look at it. To look at the matter in this way immediately gives you great strength.
D M Lloyd-Jones 3

One of the first things that a fighting soldier learns is how to protect himself in battle. Imagine a soldier in an active war zone wandering around in his T-shirt, jeans and trainers, with no protection for his head or chest, and carrying no weapon. What a superb target he would be for the enemy! Then imagine that this soldier knew that there was protection available – he was even able to list the equipment essential to successful warfare – but he hadn't bothered to act upon what he knew. The message is clear – Christians, like the vulnerable soldier, need to do more than just be aware of the existence of the armour of God: they need to realise that there is a continuous war going on and that they must wear *all* the armour *all* the time if they are to be victorious in the battle against the enemy. Paul uses similar language in the following passages.

Read 2 Corinthians 10:3,4; 1 Timothy 6:12

Q Identify the words which refer to warfare (but remember that we are not alone and it is *God's* fight).

We have a deadly enemy

Satan is never spoken of as having any independent existence. He is never spoken of as having sovereign dominion. The Bible never suggests that he has successfully cast off the government of God: he is in rebellion against it, but still held by it. That is the meaning of the petition in the Lord's prayer, 'Bring us not into temptation, but deliver us from evil.' It is a recognition of the fact that the very forces of evil in the spiritual realm are still under the government of God.
G Campbell Morgan [4]

In order that our time and efforts in warfare are properly focused, it is vital that we know who we are fighting against.

Read Ephesians 6:12,13; 1 Peter 5:8,9

Q Who is our enemy and what should our response be?

Q What descriptive names of Satan are found in these verses?

Ruler & authority of dark world
Prowling lion

Read Genesis 3:1; Matthew 4:3; John 8:44; 12:31; 2 Corinthians 4:4; 11:14; James 4:7; 1 Peter 5:8; Revelation 9:11; 12:9; 12:10.

Q Which of these terms for Satan do you find most disturbing?

We need not be anxious because our God is greater than Satan. *Take time to bring any anxieties regarding this to the Lord right now, asking him to give you the necessary discernment and appropriate response whenever and however Satan presents himself to you.*

We need protection against different kinds of attack

It is no sign, when we are under attack, that we are failing as Christians. Being terribly troubled, for example, by temptation does not mean that we are not living the Christian life properly. Indeed, in this context, it may mean the exact opposite, for it is precisely when we are what we should be that Satan turns his malevolent attention upon us most acutely.
James Philip 5

Read Ephesians 6:10–18

Q Paul counsels believers to put on 'the full armour of God'. Why is the whole armour necessary for victory?

So that I may stand firm and ready for anything the devil throws my way.

Q The various parts of the armour could be seen to be linked to various kinds of Satanic attack. Can you suggest one way in which Satan attacks Christians? Relate this to the relevant part of the armour which will defend us against this attack.

Q Are you conscious of being attacked in a particular area of your life at the present time? Don't struggle alone: pray to the Lord for help and enlist the prayer support of a trusted Christian friend.

Military instructions!

Our first weapon in battling our foe is the word of truth ... The second weapon is prayer ... The battle for the souls of men and women is really not won in the witnessing encounter or the discipling meeting, but in prayer, before we ever get into those situations. Our actions are of course necessary, but it is futile to fight without paving the way by prayer against the devil.
Jerry Bridges [6]

In Ephesians 6:10–18 we are given several encouraging commands relating to the armour of God. Four of these commands can be found in verses 10, 11, 14 and 18 – *be strong, put on, stand firm* and *pray.*

Q *Be strong* (v 10) – in whom/what are we to be strong? What do you understand by this? Why do you think this is the first command in the armour passage?

Q *Put on* (v 11) – why do we have to put the armour on? In other words, why is it not already fitted?

Q *Stand firm* (v 14) – what might be a consequence of trying to stand *before* we are strong in the Lord and equipped by him?

Q *Pray* (v 18) – what is said in this verse about prayer? Give one reason why prayer is important for the Christian in a battle context.

Personal comment

As we begin our study of armour and warfare, I'm so grateful for the opening chapters of the book of Ephesians, aren't you? They leave us in no doubt about the great spiritual blessings which belong to all those who trust in the Lord. These blessings are real and are true of you if you are a Christian. Don't forget that. However, the blessed Christian is also a battling Christian. As we go into battle with our enemy, Satan, we know what is required of us – we have been given clear commands to 'be strong in the Lord and in his mighty power'; to 'put on the full armour of God'; to 'stand firm'; and to 'always keep on praying'. So, as you put on your battle gear as outlined in Ephesians 6, remember that you fight from a position of strength – not your own, but Jesus Christ's.

The armour which the Lord provides for us is custom-made – in other words, it fits each of us perfectly. In 1 Samuel 17:38,39 we read of the shepherd-boy, David, putting on the armour of King Saul in preparation for fighting with the giant, Goliath. David very soon realises that wearing another person's armour will not be effective and he discards it. Although the same pieces of armour are to be worn by all Christians, the Lord knows that, in many ways, our experience of battle is unique to us as individuals; so let's not 'borrow' another believer's shoes or shield of faith, but acknowledge to God that we are completely dependent on him to provide armour suitable for us. Good-fitting battle gear is so vital to victorious living.

As you go through this week – whether at home, work or college – consider the many blessings which are yours as a Christian. Don't forget to thank God for all of them. Thank him also that he knows that you are weak, yet has commanded you to be strong in him. You can also thank him for providing suitable protection for you in your fight against Satan and all forms of temptation – just make sure that you obey the 'put on' command. Perhaps the Lord has given you Christian friends who will pray for you and stick by you – thank him for these people and stay close to them as you 'stand firm' for the Lord. Finally, 'pray at all times and on every occasion in the power of the Holy Spirit. Stay alert and be persistent in your prayers for all Christians everywhere' (Ephesians 6:18 – NLT).

2| Who is our enemy?

'For our struggle is not against flesh and blood, but against the rulers, against the authorities, against the powers of this dark world and against the spiritual forces of evil in the heavenly realms.'
Ephesians 6:12

Satan is real. There are hundreds of references in Scripture to Satan and his evil spirits ... The Scriptures indicate vividly that Satan is wicked, real, and powerful. Yet perhaps his greatest deception is to make people believe he doesn't exist. Someone who doesn't think Satan is real will not try to resist him.
Bill Bussard 1

What do you think might happen if soldiers went to war but didn't know who they were fighting against? Perhaps they would be so confused that they would start fighting each other, or become so discouraged by lack of victory that they would give up altogether. In every military campaign, soldiers need to know who their enemy is. The same is true for Christians. In Ephesians 6:12 we are told the focus of Christian warfare – rulers, authorities, powers and spiritual forces of evil. While Satan is our principal enemy, we must contend also with the world (1 John 2:15–17) and our own evil desires (1 Peter 2:11). The complex interrelationship between temptation and desire is perhaps best expressed in James 1:14: 'Each one is tempted when, by his own evil desire, he is dragged away and enticed.' As Paul writes in Romans 7:23, there is 'another law at work in the members of my body'. Desire is awakened and shaped by the world, whose influences Satan uses to achieve his purposes. Our enemy Satan opposes Christians with the help of his army of evil spiritual beings. In this chapter we will look at examples of Satan's activities recorded in the Bible; his current purposes in the world; and his ultimate, guaranteed destruction.

Who is Satan?

God allows Satan to retain his power and operate as a part of this world because God's sovereignty over the world is not in question. God is able to use the work even of this enemy to accomplish His own purposes – to make us stronger rather than weaker.
Timothy Warner [2]

In chapter one of this study, we saw that Satan is a master of disguise – an angel of light, a roaring lion, a dragon. In fact, he's in disguise when we first read about him in the Bible – he appears as a serpent.

Q Look at the following sample passages and write down what each tells you about our enemy.

Genesis 3:1–7,14,15

Job 1:6–12; 2:1–7

Luke 4:1–13

Q In each of these passages, notice the way that the Lord addressed Satan. What does this tell you about his position in relation to God?

Satan in perspective

There are two kingdoms in the world – God's kingdom of light, to which Christian believers belong, and Satan's kingdom of darkness, over which he exercises authority in the lives of unbelievers. Jesus refers several times (John 12:31; 14:30; and 16:11) to the devil as 'the prince of this world'. He is a prince in that he rules the minds of unconverted people, but he cannot match God's sovereignty over the universe. Paul calls the devil 'the ruler of the kingdom of the air' (Ephesians 2:2) and he reminds the Ephesian believers that, before they became Christians, they belonged to this kingdom. The idea that Paul is conveying by this phrase is that Satan is the motivating power in the lives of unbelievers – they are breathing in his ideas and values; this is the atmosphere in which they survive. He is 'the god of this age' (2 Corinthians 4:4) in that, whether or not unbelievers realise it, they have made Satan their god.

However, the Bible makes it clear that Satan's control of the world is apparent rather than real.

Q Look up the verses below and write down what is said about God's sovereignty.

Psalm 24:1

Psalm 47:2,7,8

Matthew 28:18

Q We need to remember that Satan is a defeated foe. The greatest event of all time, the death and resurrection of the Lord Jesus Christ, made certain of this. Read Colossians 2:15 and write down what it says in your own words.

Satan is limited in several ways:

He is powerful, but not as powerful as God (Matthew 28:18).

Unlike God, he is not able to be everywhere at once – this is why he needs demons to help him in his activities (Job 1:7).

Although God knows everything concerning the past, present and future (Romans 11:33–36), Satan does not.

He acts only within the boundaries of God's permission (Job 1:12).

Satan's current purposes

We must strike a Scriptural balance between the truth that Satan is a crushed, defeated foe, and the truth that he is on the prowl like a hungry lion. In other words, we must avoid the extreme of regarding him as a reigning foe, and the extreme, equally wrong, of not taking him seriously. Both extremes are condemned by Scripture. We are given abundant evidence in the New Testament of the continuing malevolent activity of Satan in human affairs. Frequently this activity is of such a nature that its satanic source is not suspected by man.

Frederick S Leahy [3]

Leahy's quote reminds us that Satan is not to be underestimated in his activities in the world. His purposes include (1) keeping unbelievers from coming to a saving faith in the Lord Jesus Christ, (2) making Christians ineffective in their daily lives, and (3) hindering God's work.

Q How does he attempt to do these things? Look up the following verses for help.

Matthew 13:19; 2 Corinthians 4:4.

2 Corinthians 2:10,11; 1 Peter 5:8,9

1 Thessalonians 2:18; James 3:13–16

A good way to respond in these situations where Satan is at work is to act on what it says in James 4:7,8: 'Submit yourselves, then, to God. Resist the devil, and he will flee from you. Come near to God and he will come near to you…'

Q In your present circumstances, what does it mean for you to submit to God? Can you identify a part of your life where you're 'doing your own thing' without paying attention to what God might think about it? Perhaps you've never seriously thought about this before. If so, *take time now* to consider these questions carefully – ask the Lord to show you what steps you need to take and then obey him!

Q Are there areas in your life where you are not resisting the devil? Be honest! God commands you to resist and will give you the strength you need if that is what you really want to do. He has also promised that if you do this, the devil will run away from you.

Q What does it mean for you to come near to God? Are you currently living so far away from him that you are unable to hear his voice and obey his commands? The Lord invites you to come to him and, if you do, he has promised that he will come near to you.

'So let God work his will in you. Yell a loud no to the devil and watch him scamper. Say a quiet yes to God and he'll be there in no time'.
James 4:7,8 *The Message* 4

As we fight against Satan and his army, we need to use the right weapons.

The war that we are engaged in is for the minds and souls of people. We've already examined the armour of Ephesians 6:10–18. Now look at the weapons of 2 Corinthians 10:3–5. What do you think are the 'weapons' referred to here?

Q What do you understand by the term 'strongholds'? Can you give an example?

Satan's future destruction

Loving heavenly Father, I praise You that Satan is a defeated foe. I rejoice that his defeat was accomplished by the Lord Jesus Christ in His sinless life, His death, burial, resurrection, and ascension into glory. I look forward to that day when the Lord Jesus Christ rules, while Satan is bound in the bottomless pit. I know that Satan will ultimately be forever consigned to the lake of fire prepared for him and his angels. I rejoice that You have given to me, in my union with the Lord Jesus Christ, complete victory over Satan today.
Mark I Bubeck 5

It is our responsibility to submit to God and to resist the devil. It is foolish to underestimate the powerful, cunning, wicked nature of our enemy, but it is also a mistake to entertain doubts about the final outcome of the spiritual battle in which all Christians are engaged. The Bible leaves us in no doubt whatsoever about the future of Satan and his demons.

Read Matthew 25:41; Romans 16:20; Jude v 6; Revelation 20:10

Q Write down what these verses tell us about their doom.

Q If you were asked to choose one of the above verses to remind you of the certainty of Satan's destruction, which would it be and why?

A personal favourite of mine is Romans 16:20 – 'The God of peace will soon crush Satan under your feet.' The address to Satan in Genesis 3:15 – 'He will crush your head' was fulfilled when Jesus died on the cross, and Satan's final defeat will be when God crushes him under the feet of believers. Take heart!

Personal comment

Do you ever think that other people are the cause of all your problems? Do you see them as enemies that you should be fighting? I don't know about you, but I sometimes forget that my real enemy is not 'flesh and blood' (Ephesians 6:12). The real enemy is Satan, a spiritual being who is evil in every way. His purposes are to stop people from becoming Christians; to prevent those who already are Christians from realising their freedom in Christ so that they will be ineffective in their day-to-day lives; and to oppose the work of God in any way he can. It seems that many Christians have an unbiblical view of Satan and are either afraid of him or dismiss his influence altogether. The Bible makes it clear that our response to Satan should be to resist him (James 4:7). He is powerful, though, and mere human beings are no match for him. We daren't tackle him relying only on our own strength – that would be both dangerous and foolish. However, we need to remember that, on the cross, Jesus won the victory over Satan and, if we are in a living relationship with Jesus, then his power is available to us. Being a child of God gives you and me authority over our enemy. In his little book, Winning Spiritual Warfare, *Neil Anderson says*

> *Before we received Christ, we were slaves to sin. But because of Christ's work on the cross, sin's power over us has been broken. Satan has no right of ownership or authority over us. He is a defeated foe, but he is committed to keeping us from realizing that. He knows he can block your effectiveness as a Christian if he can deceive you into believing that you are nothing but a product of your past, subject to sin, prone to failure, and controlled by your habits. As long as he can confuse you and blind you with his dark lies, you won't be able to see that the chains which once bound you are broken.[6]*

Let's not become intimidated by focusing too much on what Satan can do – rather, let's look at the resources which we have as Christians. In this way, we will be able to respond to Satan's temptations, accusations and deceptions with confidence.

3| The belt of truth

'Stand firm then, with the belt of truth buckled round your waist.'
Ephesians 6:14a

Truth by definition is unchanging and absolute. No matter how lib-eralised our society has become in substituting opinion for truth, people cannot change the truth about truth, no matter how loudly they proclaim their opinions or how fervently they believe them.
Mary Whelchel [1]

'I promise to tell the truth, the whole truth, and nothing but the truth.' So says the person about to give evidence in a British court of law. But what value do we really place on truth? Sadly, in many parts of today's society, truth is not generally thought to be of great importance. If it's considered at all, it's often in terms of *relative* truth: it might be true for you, but not for me; or it might have been true at one time but not now; or no one can know the truth because meaning is experienced differently from person to person. Another aspect of truth involves an individual's trustworthiness – does it matter if a person is dishonest as long as no one finds out or nobody gets hurt? What difference does it make if your behaviour is not consistent with what you say? What harm is there in the odd little white lie now and again? It is against a backdrop of questions like these that the Word of God comes to us: *'Stand firm then, with the belt of truth buckled round your waist.'*

Importance of the belt

To have on the girdle of truth – in the sense of having this holding all else in place, that is, having the girdle of truth as the integral and foundational part of all the armour, which alone keeps the soldier from being disorganised and put into disarray – means, quite sim-

ply, to allow the truth of God to be a living reality in our lives, to live by it, to act upon it, to breathe it, to let it govern our conduct and our attitude day by day, as a second nature.
James Philip 2

The Roman soldier's belt was not like the narrow fashion belts which we wear today. It was more like an apron, which was usually made of leather, and was worn to protect the lower part of the body. It was attached to the breastplate, keeping it in place, and it also held the soldier's sword. It was therefore an important piece of equipment, essential to the proper functioning of the other parts of the armour.

Read Ephesians 6:14

Q Why do you think truth is referred to here as a belt?

Q Note that the belt has to be 'buckled'. Why is this significant?

The belt as biblical truth

We are to put on knowledge of and belief in the truth of the gospel. We must embrace this truth with sincerity and a good conscience. It is precious to us; without it we will be hindered from living freely ... Truth encompasses us and gives us freedom to love, to trust, and to take a stand. We fight against an enemy of lies with a God of truth as the source of our strength.
Cynthia Heald 3

As we live and work in a society of shifting values, we need to have a firm grasp of biblical teaching. The Bible is God's revealed Word to human beings and it doesn't change; it is completely dependable and trust-worthy.

Read Psalm 119:160; Colossians 1:5

Q Write down what is said in these verses about God's revelation.

In contrast to the complete truth of the word of God, the devil is known as the father of lies. In *The Holy War* by John Bunyan, Satan is asked by one of his demons how best to attack the human mind. 'Lies, lies, lies,' answered Satan. 'We must get them to accept the lies as truth.' In order to refute the devil's lies, we need to know and apply biblical truth in our ongoing battle with him. An excellent example of this can be seen in Matthew's account of the temptation of Jesus (Matthew 4:1–11) where the Lord rebuffs each temptation by quoting passages from the book of Deuteronomy (8:3; 6:16; and 6:13). Below is a selection of Bible verses along with examples of the kind of lies the devil uses against us. Consider and match each verse and the situation or lie to which it might apply.

Verses	Lies
Matthew 28:19,20	You can't be a Christian if you did that
Luke 12:2	Jesus was just an ordinary man, nothing more
John 1:1	You can't be sure that all of the Bible is true, can you?
2 Timothy 3:16	Telling others about Jesus is not for you – if you say anything about what you believe, you'll probably mess it up
James 2:10	You'll get away with it – no one will ever know
1 John 1:8–10	It's only a little sin – it doesn't matter very much

Lies

Is there an area in your life where you are choosing to believe the devil's lies rather than God's truth? Is there a truth in the Bible that you are doubting, perhaps because you think it's not relevant to your situation? Ask the Lord to make his truth clear to you and to help you to be obedient to what he requires.

The belt as personal truthfulness/integrity

Take heed of everything contrary to truth. No longer flatter or deceive others. God's people are children who will not lie, who dare not lie, who hate and abhor lying.
Matthew Henry 4

In addition to the belt of truth illustrating the Christian's commitment to the truth of the Bible, it can also refer to a believer's personal truthfulness. Several verses in the Bible speak about the importance of being truthful.

Read Proverbs 12:22; Zechariah 8:16; Colossians 3:9

Q Write down what each says about being truthful.

Apart from telling deliberate lies, there are other ways in which we can be untruthful. Some suggestions are listed below.

◆ Exaggeration

◆ Broken promises

◆ Flattery

◆ Giving a misleading impression (deception).

Can you give an example of one of these? How might you guard against the temptation to be untruthful in this way?

If the last question makes you feel uncomfortable, will you be honest with yourself and *be specific* as you confess your lack of truthfulness to the Lord now? What other steps might you need to take if you haven't been entirely honest with another person? Consider your response prayerfully.

Read Ephesians 4:15

Q This verse tells us that the *way* we speak the truth is important. Can you suggest some practical ways of 'speaking the truth in love'?

Q Can you think of somebody in your own life to whom you need to speak the truth in love?

Read James 1:19

Q Our *response* to someone telling us the truth is also important. What does this verse say about our responsibility in this?

> *My goal is to become such a truth-lover that I willingly listen to even the hardest words. I want to deal more with issues and truth than with ego and fragile feelings. That doesn't mean I have to bow to every word of criticism that comes my way. It does mean, however, that if people bring me words that are true, I owe it to them – I owe it to me – to listen.*
> **Bill Hybels** [5]

Wearing the belt of truth also means being someone who has sincerity of heart or integrity. This is what the psalmist was talking about when he referred to 'truth in the inner parts' (Psalm 51:6). Give one example of what it means to show integrity. (A dictionary might be useful here!)

Is there an area in your life, unknown to others, which is characterised by insincerity or hypocrisy? Is there a mis-match between what you appear to be to others and what you are really like in terms of your private thoughts and attitudes? Is 'truth in the inner parts' an unreal concept to you? Take time now to be honest with yourself and, with the Lord's help, begin to deal with any insincere attitudes and behaviour patterns.

> *Integrity is important in minor matters as well as major ones. When we dig an ethical grave, it is not with a ditchdigger but with a teaspoon, one small choice at a time – a few words plagiarized, minor cheating on taxes, taking home supplies from the company, flirtations with a co-worker, white lies, or even creating a false impression to impress a neighbour.*
> Jerry White 6

Personal comment

How is your belt of truth this week? Does it fit well or are false beliefs about God or the Bible making it uncomfortable to wear? Are you falling for Satan's lies? In order to be good at telling the difference between his lies and truth, you'll need to be disciplined in reading the Word of God – the more you are familiar with it, the better the belt of truth will fit. Perhaps you haven't been truthful about something and this is making it difficult for you to fasten your belt – in fact, you have to stretch your belt to make it fit. Set the record straight and go back to wearing the belt as God intended. Without it, you are very vulnerable to Satan's lies. We saw in section one of this chapter that the belt is not worn in isolation – it is closely linked to the breastplate and the sword, for example. As we go through our study of the various pieces of armour which God gives us for our protection, we will see that they are all essential for our victory against the enemy. We are ill-equipped soldiers if we think we can have a helmet (salvation) without a breastplate (righteousness), or a shield (faith) without a belt (truth).

In the Old Testament, God is referred to as 'the God of truth' (Psalm 31:5), while in John 14:6, Jesus says of himself 'I am the way, the truth and the life.' The apostle John describes the Lord as being 'full of grace and truth' (John 1:14) and the Holy Spirit is described as the Spirit of truth (John 14:17; 15:26; 16:13). How good it is to know that when we put on the belt of truth as a protective piece of battle equipment we are putting on the character of God! In everyday life, there are many attacks on our hold of the truth – these might include doubts about the relevance of God's Word (does it really apply to me in this situation?); suggestions that believing in the existence of absolute truth is outdated (can I really believe that the Bible is true in today's society?); temptations to be less than truthful in our interactions with others (nobody will know if I'm not entirely truthful – it's no big deal... is it?); and enticements to compromise our integrity (it's not my problem that the cashier in the DIY store gave me change from £20 when I only gave her £10).

In every situation you meet this week, will you wear the belt of truth? Will you make sure that your belt is buckled ie set firmly and securely in place, round your waist? Do you long to have 'truth in the inner parts', ie a direct link between thoughts, motives, desires on the one hand and speech and behaviour on the other? We're engaged in battle with a subtle, deceitful and powerful enemy, but if we live under the protection of God's armour, we can be victorious. Take courage from 1 John 4:4: 'the Spirit who lives in you is greater than the spirit who lives in the world' (NLT). Read again Ephesians 6:10–18. Become very familiar with this passage of Scripture, allowing its truth to shape you into the person God wants you to be.

4| The breastplate of righteousness

'Stand firm then ... with the breastplate of righteousness in place'
Ephesians 6:14b

This breastplate has to be the righteousness of Jesus Christ. Our self-righteousness will never protect us. If you think Satan is intimidated by the good things you've done, or the good life you lead, forget it. The Bible tells us that all our righteousness is as filthy rags, so trying to impress Satan with what we've done, or who we are, is like wearing tissue paper for a breastplate. Self-righteousness will never protect you. Only the righteousness of Jesus Christ will avail.
Mary Whelchel [1]

The invitation card read 'Carriages at midnight'. This conjured up images of wealthy Victorian ladies and gentlemen being transported home after a high-society evening. The reality was much more mundane – merely modern-day parents going home in cars and taxis after enjoying a school fund-raising dinner! The term 'carriages' seemed quaintly out of place and might have been more appropriate a hundred years ago. 'Righteousness' is another term which is not used a lot today. It is almost as if it, too, should belong in the past. Sadly, there are many who would like nothing better than to relegate righteousness to another time and place. The word simply means 'rightness' – being in a right relationship with God and living in a right way before God and people. In this chapter, we will consider the importance of the breastplate in the soldier's armour; the breastplate as the righteousness of Christ; and the breastplate as a right lifestyle.

The importance of the breastplate

As we choose righteousness and reject sin, then we are putting on the breastplate of righteousness. And if we have this piece of armour in place, then we can stand firm with confidence in the face of spiritual foes. But if we toy with sin, then the breastplate of righteousness drops to the ground, and suddenly we are vulnerable. Suddenly we are subject to damage and to harm. Put on the breastplate of righteousness by choosing each day to be obedient to Christ.
Cheryl Sneeringer [2]

No Roman soldier would be properly dressed for battle without his breastplate. The breastplate was made of metal and rested on the shoulders, going from the neck to the thighs, covering both the front *and* back of the body. As such, this piece of armour protected vital organs such as heart, lungs, liver.

Read Ephesians 6:14

Q Why do you think this passage refers to righteousness as a breastplate?

Read Isaiah 59:15b–17

Q This passage prophesies the atoning work of Christ. Whose righteousness sustained him?

Q Whose righteousness was his breastplate?

Read 1 Thessalonians 5:8

Q This is Paul's reading of these verses in Isaiah. Whose faith and love should we put on as our breastplate?

Q What reason does Paul give for our wearing this piece of armour?

The breastplate as Christ's righteousness

Let us not show the bare breast of our righteousness to the tempter, but rather the righteousness of God Himself, imputed to us and received by faith. This breastplate was purchased by Christ at a dear rate; none are His soldiers who have not put it on.
T Croskery [3]

Did you know that God is very much into the business of 'give and take'? When we become Christians, he *takes* away our sins and *gives* us the righteousness of Christ in exchange! This means that we are no longer condemned by God for sins which we committed in the past *(Romans 8:1)* because when he looks at us, he sees us wearing Christ's righteousness. Isn't that incredible? It's like receiving an injection of cash into a bank account that is severely in debt: suddenly, the debt is wiped out and the account is in credit. In the same way, God credits Christ's righteousness to us.

Read Romans 3:21–24; Philippians 3:8,9

Q Write down what these verses say about this righteousness.

Have you been accepted by God through faith in the Lord Jesus Christ? Have you received his righteousness in exchange for your sins? If you can answer 'yes' to these questions, *take time now* to thank the Lord that this is true of you. If your answer is 'no', think about your need to be put right with God by turning to him in repentance and faith. You may wish to speak to your group leaders about this – they will be able to help and direct you in this very important matter. Alternatively you may wish to look at one or more of the following:

Journey Into Life by Norman Warren, Kingsway, 1964

Why Jesus? by Nicky Gumbel, Alpha Publications, 1991

Right With God by John Blanchard, Banner of Truth, 1988

Read Zechariah 3

Q Here we read of Joshua the high priest standing before the angel of the Lord. Read verses 1–5. In what way(s) is this an illustration of the Christian receiving Christ's righteousness?

Q Verse 1 records that Satan stood beside Joshua to accuse him. Using the surrounding verses to aid your answer, what do you think was the nature of the accusation?

Q In what way can the breastplate of righteousness help you when you are attacked in this way?

The breastplate as a right lifestyle

Believers are called to holiness. Though it may sound like a stained-glass word, evoking the image of soft organ music and whispered prayers, holiness simply means 'to be set apart' – set apart from sin, set apart to God. Being set apart has to come from the heart.
Jan Silvious [4]

God gives us Christ's righteousness when we become Christians – but he doesn't stop there. He also gives us the desire to live in a way that is pleasing to him. Our thoughts, attitudes, motives and behaviour begin a life-long process of change.

Read Romans 6:12,13; Ephesians 4:22–24

Q Read the verses above and paraphrase what the writer is saying.

Q The above verses emphasise the necessity of a Christian living a right-eous life – why is this important?

Read Zechariah 3

Q Read again the account of Joshua the high priest. In the light of verses 1–5 what is the significance of the command in verse 7?

It is in everyday living that we are most vulnerable to Satan's attacks. We need to make sure that we are not relying on our own moral goodness or strength of character to protect us, but are relying on the Lord to such an extent that his righteousness becomes more and more infused into our character. We have already seen that the soldier's breastplate protects the vital organs. One of these is the heart. In everyday life, in order to keep a healthy heart, we need to give attention to three main things. These are diet, exercise and rest. Let's now consider how these three things can be relevant to maintaining a healthy 'spiritual heart'.

Q A healthy diet protects the heart by preventing its arteries from becoming clogged up. Match up the following verses with the appro-priate example of a wholesome spiritual diet.

Verses	Examples
John 7:37	Feasting on God's Word
Acts 2:42–46	Filling one's mind with good thoughts
Acts 17:11	Meeting with other believers
Philippians 4:8	Drinking the water of the Spirit

Choose at least one of the above principles and say how you plan to apply it to your life this week.

Q Exercise protects the heart by increasing its endurance level and making it strong. Match up the following verses with the appropriate example of spiritual exercise.

Verses	Examples
John 14:15	Repentance
Hebrews 11:6	Obedience
Hebrews 13:15	Faith
1 John 1:9	Praise

Choose at least one of the above principles and say how you plan to apply it to your life this week.

Q Physical rest protects the heart by limiting the demands upon it. Match up the following verses with the appropriate example of spiritual rest.

Verses	Examples
Psalm 37:7	Spending time with the Lord
Psalm 77:11,12	Reflecting on what God has done
Matthew 6:33,34	Patient trust
Mark 6:31	Freedom from worry

Choose at least one of the above principles and say how you plan to apply it to your life this week.

There are times in every Christian's life when it's uncomfortable to wear the breastplate of righteousness because wrong thoughts and behaviour patterns prevent it from fitting properly. The descriptions below could be considered examples of this. (This is *not* an exhaustive list – you might wish to add some more of your own!)

- ◆ Careless viewing habits (Psalm 101:2,3)

- ◆ Lack of personal discipline (Proverbs 5:23)

- ◆ Self-absorption (1 Corinthians 10:24)

- ◆ Unforgiving spirit (Matthew 6:15)

- ◆ Complaining attitude (Philippians 2:14)

- ◆ Inappropriate speech (Colossians 3:8)

- ◆ Lustful desires (Matthew 5:27,28).

Choose one of the above and think about how you would assist a person trying to deal with this particular problem.

Is there an area of your life where the breastplate of righteousness has slipped from its proper position? Are you struggling because you have failed to resist the devil's attacks? Affirm once again that you have been washed and are covered with Christ's righteousness. Then, with the Holy Spirit's help, through prayer, put on the breastplate of a righteous, holy lifestyle. You don't have to give in to Satan's attacks, fierce as they may be, because God has provided you with an escape route (1 Corinthians 10:13). Don't let yesterday's failures in right living hinder your progress in right-eousness today – apologise to God for your failures and, with his forgiveness, start afresh.

> *Righteous character and actions are ... part of the breastplate. When we consistently say no to our sinful desires, the devil gets no opportunity to gain a foothold in our lives (Ephesians 4:17–32).*
> Warren and Ruth Myers 5

Personal comment

I'm so glad that God provides this breastplate as protection for the heart – that part of us which Bible writers considered to be the root of the emotions, desires and thoughts. Genetically, my heart is very vulnerable. Both of my parents died of heart disease, so, as far as is possible, I should take all necessary steps to minimise the probability of heart disease in my own life. I need to give particular attention to correct diet, responsible exercise and adequate rest. What is true of me physically is also true of me spiritually – I need to protect my heart! I hope you found the suggestions in section 3 of this study to be helpful. A healthy spiritual diet will include feasting on God's Word; incorporating godly friends into my life; and filling my mind with good thoughts. Appropriate spiritual exercise involves daily repentance; obedience to God's Word and will; and offerings of praise to him, even when (and perhaps especially when) I don't feel like it. In my busy lifestyle, where many responsibilities compete for my attention, it is so important to practise the discipline of rest – to reflect on my eternal security as a believer in the Lord Jesus Christ; to take time to be holy by resting from things which would distract me from this goal; and to receive rest from guilt-ridden emotions as my breastplate of righteousness protects me from Satan's accusing voice.

God has provided all the equipment necessary for us to live a life that is pleasing to him. He has given us his Word, the Bible, to be our daily guide; he lives in us by his Holy Spirit, empowering and directing us; and he provides custom-made armour for the spiritual battle that we, as Christians, are all engaged in. We have to make sure that we put this armour on and make ongoing checks that it is still in place. Wearing the armour, though, does not prevent Satan from attacking us; he will attack – you can depend upon it – but wearing God's armour will protect us from the harm and destruction that the devil wants to bring into our lives. Wearing the breastplate of righteousness means that we are covered by the righteousness of Jesus Christ – Satan hates to be reminded of that. It also involves getting rid of anything in our lives which is not right. Are you holding on to some wrong way of thinking or living which makes it difficult for the breastplate to fit properly? If so, then you're making it easy for Satan to wound you. If there is anything in your life which you know is not right, then confront it and get rid of it. You'll find that your breastplate will then be much more comfortable to wear.

No individual can prescribe exactly how you should wear your breastplate of righteousness. But do give serious consideration to this piece of the armour – with the Holy Spirit's help, begin to highlight specific areas of your life where chinks in your armour are allowing Satan to strike home. 'Stand firm then … with the breastplate of righteousness in place.'

5| The shoes of peace

'... and with your feet fitted with the readiness that comes from the gospel of peace.'
Ephesians 6:15

We feel most comfortable in our old shoes, for they fit the foot so well, but they will wear out at last: these shoes of my text are old, yet ever new. The everlasting gospel yields us everlasting peace. The good news from heaven never grows stale. The man who wears the preparation of the gospel of peace was comforted by it when he was young, and it still cheers him in his later days. It made him a good traveller when he first set out, and it will protect his last footsteps when he crosses the river Jordan and climbs the celestial hills.
Charles Spurgeon 1

Some years ago, there was an advert on television where a man gave a stimulus word to a woman and she had to respond to him with the first word that came into her head. This continued for a while until her response was the name of the product being advertised. Imagine if the stimulus word was 'peace', would you be surprised if her response was 'feet'? I think I would be because I usually associate peace with my heart or mind (see Philippians 4:7) and not with my feet! In Ephesians 6:15, however, the apostle Paul says we are to have our 'feet fitted with the readiness that comes from the gospel of peace'. Taking the Roman soldier as our model once again, we will look in this chapter at the importance of wearing proper footwear as we battle with the enemy.

The importance of the shoes

The man whose feet are well shod is not afraid to go through thick or thin, foul or fair, stones or straws; all are alike to him. But the barefooted man, or the one with fragile shoes, shrinks when his feet touch the mud, and shrieks when he stumbles on a sharp stone. Thus when the will and heart of a person are ready for any work, he is shod and armed against any trouble he must go through to complete it.
William Gurnall 2

The Roman soldier did not fight barefoot. His footwear consisted of sandals, which were essentially soles with leather straps firmly tied round his ankles. On the underside of these soles were hob nails or studs which enabled the soldier to maintain a firm footing and to *stand* without wavering. Sandals also allowed the soldier to *move* around so that he could respond appropriately to the various attacks of the enemy. The sandals were light and didn't weigh him down – an essential element in enabling him to adapt his fighting position with ease. A final point about the importance of the shoes is that *both* feet had to be shod – this was vital for the soldier to maintain *balance*.

Q In addition to standing, movement and balance, can you think of any other function for the footwear of the Roman soldier?

Q What spiritual lesson can we learn from this?

The shoes as the gospel of peace

Knowing the one true gospel is paramount, for if you have a false gospel, your beliefs about the person of the Lord Jesus Christ – the only Son of God – will be wrong. If you are wrong on the gospel, you

will not understand the work of Jesus Christ and why He died. Likewise, your views of the needs of mankind will be erroneous. Christ died for our sins. Man is a sinner. The world needs to know the gospel, the good news that no one has to stay the way he is. Jesus Christ has paid the price and has released the power that can transform lives. That is the gospel.
Warren W Wiersbe 3

In order for Christians to stand firm in spiritual warfare, they need to know what the gospel of peace is. In 1 Corinthians 15:1–5 we have a good description of this gospel.

Read 1 Corinthians 15:1–5

Q Summarise the main principles.

The apostle Paul emphasises the importance of the Christian standing firmly on the gospel of peace.

Read 1 Corinthians 15:58; 16:13

Q Write down what each verse says about how we should face the enemy in battle.

Q What encouragement might you give to a Christian who is beginning to slip as far as their belief in the gospel is concerned?

The gospel of peace is the gospel of the God of peace (Hebrews 13:20,21). As a result of believing, we have peace with God; we experience the peace of God; we are at peace with ourselves; and we are commanded to live in peace with other people. Match up the following references with each of these aspects of the Christian's peace.

Verses	Aspects of peace
Acts 24:16	Peace with God
Romans 5:1,2	Peace of God
Romans 12:18	Peace with ourselves
Ephesians 4:3	Peace with other Christians
Philippians 4:6,7	Peace with all people

Are you standing firmly on the gospel of peace? Make sure you don't believe another 'gospel' which says that salvation is automatically yours because your parents or friends are Christians; or because you do good works or try your best. Ask the Lord to remind you of his gospel of peace and thank him for it.

The shoes as readiness for action

The motto of the Boy Scouts and Girl Guides, 'Be prepared', is a good one. If we are prepared for something, we are less likely to be caught off guard. Similarly, the gospel of peace brings us into a state of 'preparation' or 'readiness'. There are many things for which the gospel of peace prepares us. It prepares us to stand firm in the tough times. It also prepares us to be balanced in our emphasis on the Word of God. Furthermore, it prepares us to be adaptable in our fight with the enemy. Finally, it prepares us to share the good news with those who are not Christians.

1 Be ready to stand firm in the tough times:

Having peace *with* God and knowing the peace *of* God in our everyday experience does not mean that we'll always be free from difficulties and suffering. Satan loves to attack the Christian's peace of mind, resulting sometimes in feelings of anxiety and dread that might be difficult to explain, with thoughts and emotions in turmoil. Look up the following verses and record how they can help Christians to keep a firm grip on life.

Read Psalm 4:8; Isaiah 26:3,4; Colossians 3:15

Q If you were asked to choose one of the above references as a help in time of trouble, which would it be and why?

Memorise your chosen verse and turn your attention to it every day until your next Bible study meeting. Look for ways in which you can apply it to your own circumstances.

2 Be ready to take a balanced view of God's Word:

Can you imagine a soldier, fighting with the enemy, wearing only one shoe? He would very quickly be knocked off balance! Satan would love us to be unbalanced, and we can become like this if we overemphasise some aspect of biblical truth at the expense of other teachings given in the Bible. For example, a belief in both the love and holiness of God is vital to a correct understanding of his nature, and we become unbalanced if we think that one is more important than the other – we end up wearing only one shoe, as it were. Select the word(s) in the verses below which suggest the importance of maintaining a balanced view of God's Word.

Read 2 Timothy 3:16,17

Are your feet resting on the *whole* of God's Word? Or are you giving more attention and obedience to those teachings which have greater 'appeal' for you? Don't limp through life wearing only one shoe!

3 Be ready to be adaptable:

The Roman soldier's footwear gave him not only stability and balance but ease of movement. The material was sufficiently lightweight to enable him to move from one part of the battlefield to another whenever the enemy changed its method and place of attack. Although Christians must not be moved in their belief in the gospel of peace, they must show readiness to adapt their strategies to Satan's changing tactics.

Read Genesis 39:7–12

Q In this passage we read of three different responses which Joseph made when Potiphar's wife tried to seduce him. List the responses beside the verses:

Verses 7–9

Verse 10

Verses 11,12

Q In what way(s) can any or all of these adaptable responses be useful in your own battle with the enemy?

> *The one thing that is hindering the work of God most today is an unwillingness to change on the part of many Christians. This does not mean that we should change shoes. We must never change the gospel. However, at times it is necessary to change our tactics and approach in sharing the Good News.*
> **Warren W Wiersbe** [4]

4 Be ready to share the good news:

Part of winning battles involves advancing into enemy territory to gain new ground. Here, as in the other areas of readiness, we need the protection of the shoes of the gospel of peace.

Read Matthew 28:19,20; Luke 8:38,39; 1 Peter 3:15

Q Write down how these verses encourage us to share the good news of
Jesus Christ with others.

How ready in recent times have you been to tell a family member, a friend,
a work colleague, or a neighbour about the good news of peace with God?
Ask the Lord to give you the opportunity, the compassion and the
courage to share with others what your relationship with him means to
you – and then trust him for the outcome.

> *Before you go out to preach the gospel to sinners and teach the gospel
> to saints, make sure you are protected by the peace of God! Your heart
> and mind will be a target of the enemy's attacks of fear and anxiety.
> He will try to knock you off balance and keep your focus inward
> rather than outward. Let Philippians 4:6–9 be your stability today.*
> Rich Miller 5

Personal comment

*I love shoes. In fact, I think there are more shoes in my wardrobe than
anything else! My love affair with footwear goes back many years and there
are certain shoes which bring back vivid memories. I remember feeling so
proud at the age of five when I learnt to tie up my school shoes all by myself!
A few years later I won an art competition and used the prize money to buy a
pair of high-fashion sandals. In my late teens, two favourite items of footwear
were black, knee-high boots with a strawberry design on the sides, and a pair
of clogs, coloured green, yellow and orange. But one item of footwear stands
out in my memory – this was a pair of black Wellington boots. I must have
been about five or six years old at the time and these boots were firm
favourites. Looking through old photographs recently, the black 'wellies' could
be seen on my feet more often than not – even with my shorts on a hot
summer's day! I forget the number of times that I was sternly warned not to
run while wearing these boots. 'They are not built for running,' I was told.
'You'll trip and fall if you do.' However, anxious to get home for something to
eat after being out playing all day, I ran wearing the 'wellies', and promptly
tripped over a metal man-hole cover, falling onto the road – the blood-*

stained face told its own story. The lessons to be learned from this? Firstly, I chose to be disobedient. I was told by my mother not to run in these boots. She knew that I could get hurt if I didn't pay attention to her instructions. How ready are you to obey the words in Ephesians 6:15, instructing you to have 'your feet fitted with the readiness that comes from the gospel of peace'? Being obedient to the Lord's command is essential if you are to avoid serious injury in the battle. Secondly, the 'wellies' didn't allow me to have a proper grip on the ground as I ran. Do you grip the truth of the Bible with confidence? Are you unmoveable when it comes to gospel truth or do you find yourself slipping anchor in the face of Satan's attacks? Thirdly, the boots weighed me down – I couldn't be as agile as I might have been had I been wearing footwear which was appropriate for running. Is there anything which is weighing you down in your Christian life? Are you carrying 'excess baggage' which limits your freedom in Christ? If so, pay attention to Hebrews 12:1 which tells us to 'throw off everything that hinders and the sin that so easily entangles, and let us run with perseverance the race marked out for us'. How glad I am to add the shoes of peace to my collection of footwear!

6| The shield of faith

'In addition to all of this, take up the shield of faith, with which you can extinguish all the flaming arrows of the evil one.'
Ephesians 6:16

Taking the shield of faith, then, is responding to the things the devil hurls at us by the quick application of what we believe about God and His Word, the Bible. When Satan sends his 'fiery darts' in our direction, we can either stand and lament the fact that we are being attacked, or quickly raise the shield of faith and remind ourselves that the devil is a liar from the beginning, and because we are redeemed by the blood of Christ, he has no legal or moral right to taunt us. But believing that is not enough; it must be acted on – and acted on quickly.
Selwyn Hughes [1]

Did you ever watch The Phantom Menace, part of the Star Wars series? At one point in the film the 'goodies' erected a huge transparent shield, which covered them like a dome, in the hope that the weapons of the 'baddies' wouldn't be able to penetrate it. We have the protection of a shield available to us too. In fact, we're given the command: '…take up the shield of faith, with which you can extinguish all the flaming arrows of the evil one' (Ephesians 6:16). This verse is a call to action and is one of my favourite parts of the armour. I love the encouragement which tells me that, with this shield of faith, I can extinguish all of the flaming arrows which Satan hurls at me.

The importance of the shield

We are equipped with a shield of faith to deflect Satan's blows. That shield of faith is our belief that God's word is true and that we can rely on it. When thoughts condemn us, we can say, 'I recognize you, Satan, as the one who has shot a flaming arrow into my mind and disrupted my peace and joy. I will not stand for it any longer. I raise my shield of faith and say, "If God is for us, who can be against us?" And I remind you that you are the one who is defeated and I am victorious in Christ. My sin is covered by His blood, and you have no right there. So be gone ... and be gone now!'
Jan Silvious [2]

The shield used by the Roman soldier was large, measuring about 120 centimetres by 75 centimetres, and covered most of his body. The shield was also moveable – the soldier could manoeuvre it in response to the enemy's attacks as and when necessary. An important fact about the shield was that it was made of wood and covered in cloth and leather. The leather was often dipped in water so that the flaming arrows shot by the enemy would, on impact with the shield, be extinguished. These fiery darts were sharp-pointed pieces of wood or metal hurled by the opposing army. The points of these darts were covered with inflammable material which was set alight when it was time to attack. These flaming arrows would be hurled in all directions to cause confusion and, if they penetrated a gap in the soldier's armour, he would be burned, making it difficult for him to continue fighting effectively. This approach was used to inflict initial injury and weakness before the all-out mass attack of the enemy.

Q Why do you think that faith in God is described as a shield?

Read Psalm 91:4

Q What comfort do you get from this?

The shield as individual faith

Remember that faith extinguishes every one of Satan's arrows, and when we become stronger and stronger in our faith, he is less able to find vulnerable places to aim at. And how do we build our faith? Faith comes by hearing and hearing by the Word of God. There are some basics of the Christian life for which there are no substitutes, and one is submerging yourself in God's Word. If you're not doing that, don't expect to be victorious against your enemy – he'll get through to you easily. If you think you're too busy, you've just opened yourself up to defeat.
Mary Whelchel [3]

Hebrews 11:6 says that 'without faith it is impossible to please God'. It is not the size of our faith which is of primary importance, but the object of our faith – our faith and trust have to be in God, both for salvation and for his ongoing help in living out Christian principles in our everyday circumstances.

Read Psalm 3:3; 18:30; 28:7; 84:11; 119:114

Q These passages all speak of God as our shield. Select one which you find particularly meaningful and share with your group the reasons for your choice.

In Ephesians 6:16 we are told precisely what the purpose of the shield of faith is – to 'extinguish all the flaming arrows of the evil one'. (Note that this is the only piece of armour which has an explicit consequence attached to it.) An important starting point in being able to hold up the shield of faith effectively is to recognise what these flaming arrows are. The following table gives verses which contain examples of the kind of arrows which the devil hurls at us. Identify the relevant flaming arrows from the list and write down how they can be extinguished. (Flaming arrows: doubt, feelings of inadequacy, discouragement, fear, anxiety.)

Verses	Flaming arrow	How extinguished
Isa 41:10/ John 14:27		
Ps 94:19/ Phil 4:6,7		
Exod 6:9/ Ps 42:5		
Gen 3:1/ Matt 21:21		
Exod 4:10/ Phil 4:13		

Are you able to share with the rest of your group a recent incident in your own experience when using the shield of faith helped you to extinguish any of the Satanic darts mentioned in these verses?

Have any of these flaming arrows pierced or burned you recently? Did you recognise them as such? Is your shield of faith made up of confidence in the Word of God? Are you sufficiently familiar with relevant Bible verses to build them into a shield of defence? Take time to consider these questions prayerfully, asking the Lord to help you to detect the source of these painful attacks, and hold up your shield of faith, making sure that it is not a cardboard shield of your own making, but is built of trust in God and his Word.

The shield as corporate faith

When tempted to quarrel and divide, all believers need to take careful stock of their motivations. Do latent attitudes of envy, competitiveness, or one-upmanship drive the situation and need to be resisted? The Spirit calls us to a visible unity. Let's not challenge that unity lightly.
Clinton E Arnold [4]

The large shield used by the Roman soldier was constructed in such a way that its bevelled edges could link up with the shields of the other soldiers in the army. This meant that the soldiers could stand shoulder to shoulder, their shields interlocking, forming a solid wall against the barrage of enemy attack. The soldiers in the row behind offered further protection for the backs of the soldiers in front. In what way is this an illustration of the faith of Christians?

Read Ephesians 4:13; 1 Peter 5:8,9

Q These verses talk about being united in faith with other Christians. What encouragement do you receive from this?

Q Why is unity with other Christians important?

Q In what way(s) do we 'miss out' if we think we can fight the battle on our own?

How willing are you to work with other Christians? Do you see the benefits for God's glory and your own good if you 'lock shields' with other believers? Take time to seek the Lord's perspective on this and desire to be obedient to him.

There are some flaming arrows which are more likely to be fired at a body of believers rather than at an individual Christian. Read the following verses and match them up with the appropriate arrows. As in the previous section, use the verses to suggest ways in which the arrows can be extinguished. (Flaming arrows: confusion, jealousy, anger, discord.)

Verses	Flaming arrow	How extinguished
1Cor 3:3/ Phil 2:3b		
Gal 5:20/ John 13:35		
Gal 1:7/ Eph 1:17,18		
Matt 5:22/ Eph 4:26,27		

Q Do these verses give you a clearer understanding of why there is some-times disharmony among Christians? Try to share with the rest of your group the reason for your answer.

Q In what practical way(s) will you hold up the shield of faith in order to deflect such destructive arrows aimed at your fellowship with other Christians?

If you have personally allowed any of the flaming arrows mentioned in this chapter to sour your fellowship with one or more Christians, take time now to confess this to the Lord. This might involve seeking out the person(s) concerned in an attempt to bring about reconciliation (Matthew 5:23,24).

Personal comment

Have you ever wondered why God provided a shield of faith? After all, we already have a belt, a breastplate, shoes, a helmet and a sword. Why have armour to cover the armour? I think that the shield of faith exists because it's such a versatile addition to our armour. What good is a belt of truth if you don't have faith in the truth of the Bible? Or a breastplate of righteousness if you don't exercise faith in the righteousness of Christ? Or shoes of peace if you don't take on board the gospel by faith...? Faith is very important in the

Christian's life and Satan knows it. That's why he loves to attack your faith by firing missiles of doubt, for example. If he can get you to doubt the object of your faith – God himself – then he's on to a winner. Fear is a closely related missile and can cause havoc in your life. In her very helpful book, Tame Your Fears,[5] Carol Kent suggests there are five types of fears: fear of things that haven't happened – yet; fear of being vulnerable; fear of abandonment; fear of truth; and fear of making wrong choices. I recommend this book for those of you who really struggle with fear in your lives. Other flaming arrows are perhaps less obvious and for that reason we need to be particularly alert. We cannot stop the flaming arrows being fired at us, but we can be obedient to the command to take up the shield of faith. I find it so encouraging that there is a promise added to the use of this piece of armour – all the flaming arrows of the evil one can be extinguished if I hold up the shield of faith which God has provided for me. It is so good to know that God has equipped me, and every Christian, in such a complete way. Despite the ferocity of some of Satan's attacks, we need to remind ourselves that we are on the winning side.

7| The helmet of salvation

'Take the helmet of salvation'
Ephesians 6:17a

A helmet guards the head and protects the eyes. This part of
Christian armour, therefore, is obviously something for the mind,
and the thoughts. The meaning in brief appears to be something like
this: a mind constantly preoccupied with thoughts of our great salva-
tion is kept safe from the onslaughts of the enemy.
James Philip [1]

The police and ambulance crew looked down at the seriously injured motor cyclist. 'If only he had been wearing his helmet,' one of them said, 'his injuries might not have been so bad…' Do you think it's foolish to ride a motor bike at speed without wearing a helmet? Do you think it's any less foolish to step out into the rush of the day without your helmet of salvation? Every time we fail to protect our minds with this God-given piece of armour, we run the risk of serious damage to our thought life – we need to guard what goes into our minds and the helmet of salvation helps us do this. In this chapter, we're going to look at the importance of the helmet; the relationship of the helmet to salvation; and the helmet as protection for our minds.

The importance of the helmet

The true helmet of hope must come from the heavenly arsenal. You
must go to the divine storehouse, for to God belongs salvation, and
the hope of salvation must be given to you by His free grace. A hope

of salvation is not purchasable. Our great King does not sell His armour but gives it freely to all who enlist. From head to foot the soldiers of the cross are arrayed by grace.
Charles Spurgeon 2

The Roman soldier's helmet was usually made of bronze or iron and often lined with a soft spongy material like felt. Some sources suggest that the helmets were more like caps and were made of leather, reinforced with ornamental plates of metal. Additional ornamentation was provided by the crest or plume at the apex of the helmet. The helmet was held in place by a leather strap and, in some cases, the eyes could be covered by a visor which was attached via hinges to the main part of the helmet. In this way, the helmet protected two vital parts of the soldier's body – his head and his eyes. A blow to the head could be fatal, and damage inflicted on his eyes could result in him having to leave the battlefield. The helmet was never far away from the soldier – it might have been slung over his shoulder when no active fighting was taking place or at other times it would have been attached to his belt. At the first sign of active fighting, the soldier would put on his helmet, grab his shield and reach for his sword. His belt, breastplate and shoes would already be on his body.

Read Ephesians 6:17a

Q Why do you think that salvation is compared to a helmet?

Read Isaiah 59:15b–17

Q These verses prophesy the atoning work of Christ. Who worked salvation?

Q Why did the Lord need to wear armour?

Read 1 Thessalonians 5:8

Q This is Paul's reading of these verses in Isaiah. What reason does Paul give for our wearing this piece of armour?

The helmet and salvation

As we choose to adopt an eternal perspective, fixing our minds on what God has promised for the future, then we have shielded our minds from Satan's blows to the head. The helmet of salvation refers to the implications of our salvation, to the sure and certain knowledge that we have eternal life with Christ. The helmet of salvation is the eternal perspective we have as we fix our hope on what God has promised for our future.
Cheryl Sneeringer [3]

A Christian's salvation is past, present and future. Several references in the Bible bring this out, but one verse which combines all three tenses is John 5:24, where Jesus says: 'I tell you the truth, whoever hears my word and believes him who sent me has eternal life [present] and will not be condemned [future]; he has crossed over from death to life [past].' Whenever Satan encourages you to doubt the reality of your salvation, you can 'take the helmet of salvation' and remind him that:

◆ You have already been saved from the penalty of sin – Jesus has borne your condemnation and there is now none for you if you are trusting in him (Romans 8:1).

◆ You are presently being saved from the power of sin in that you are being made more like Jesus by the power of the Holy Spirit within you (2 Corinthians 3:17, 18).

◆ You will one day be saved from the presence of sin when you go to be with Jesus in heaven (Revelation 21:27).

Take time to read John 5:24 several times. As you consider the words of Jesus, give thanks that, as a Christian, the truths of this verse apply to you.

It is the idea of future salvation which links the helmet in Ephesians 6:17 with the one in 1 Thessalonians 5:8 – 'the *hope* of salvation as a helmet'. Read the following verses and match them up with the various examples of the Christian's hope of future salvation.

Verses	Hope of future salvation
John 14:2,3	Hope of eternal security
Romans 8:38,39	Hope of being like the Lord
2 Corinthians 4:16-18	Hope of Jesus appearing
Ephesians 5:25-27	Hope of glory
Titus 2:13	Hope of being presented to Christ without sin
1 John 3:2,3	Hope of an eternal home

The helmet as protection for our thinking

Protecting our minds with the salvation which we have from Christ means that we don't allow anything into our minds which contradicts or violates or offends that salvation. Anything that is not in harmony with our commitment to Jesus Christ and the salvation he has given us should not penetrate our mind.
Mary Whelchel 4

In addition to providing us with a certain hope for the future, the helmet of salvation is also relevant to life here and now. One of its main functions is to protect our minds from wrong thinking. Remember that the Roman soldier's helmet offered protection for his head. In the same way, the helmet of salvation offers protection for the Christian's mind.

Read 2 Corinthians 10:3–5

Q Here Paul uses battle language as he urges us to 'take captive every thought to make it obedient to Christ'. What do you think is meant by this statement?

Q Why is it important that *every* thought is included?

Read Romans 12:2; Ephesians 4:23; 1 Peter 1:13

Q These verses all refer to the mind. Write down what each says about this important part of our selves.

Q If you were asked to choose one of the above verses to commit to memory this week, which one would it be and why?

A Bible verse which I find very helpful regarding right thinking is Philippians 4:8. In the New Living Translation it reads 'fix your thoughts on what is true and honourable and right. Think about things that are pure and lovely and admirable'. Putting on the helmet of salvation can help you to make this verse a reality in your life. In the following table, give examples of these different kinds of thinking, along with their opposites. Don't worry if you find it difficult to think of examples for some of them – just do what you can. I've given a possible answer for the first one.

True thinking	Untrue thinking
Thoughts which are factually correct eg God loves me; God is good; God is holy.	Worrying about what might happen
	Thinking that something is true, even though I don't have evidence to back it up.
Honourable thinking	**Dishonourable thinking**
add comment	
Right thinking	**Wrong thinking**
add comment	
Pure thinking	**Impure thinking**
add comment	

Lovely thinking	Unlovely thinking
add comment	
Admirable thinking	Unworthy thinking
add comment	

Write down examples of wrong thinking which you can identify with personally in your thought life but which you would rather not share with the rest of your group. Please make this a matter of prayer between yourself and the Lord. He is the only one who can clean up wrong thoughts and bring about right thinking in your mind.

In talking about the Roman soldier's helmet near the start of this chapter, I mentioned that some helmets had a visor which could be pulled down to protect the eyes during the battle. This reminds me that the helmet of salvation not only guards our minds from wrong thinking, but also gives protection for our eyes (see Job 31:1–3) and ears. Why is it important to guard what we see and hear?

What are you allowing yourself to see and hear which has a damaging effect on your thought life? Are there any TV programmes, videos, films, web sites, books or magazines that you need to avoid in order to practise right thinking? Please *take time now* to bring this matter to the Lord so that you can eliminate wrong choices and make right choices with regard to your viewing material.

Garbage in, garbage out. Please remember that you are responsible for what you allow into your mind, and whatever gets in becomes the fodder for your thought life. You can't allow sewage into your drinking water and not expect to get very sick. You can't allow garbage into your mind and not expect to have some very sick thoughts as a result.
Mary Whelchel 5

Personal comment

In this chapter, we've looked at the helmet of salvation and how this protects us from Satanic attack aimed at our thoughts regarding our eternal security. We also noted that the helmet protects our minds and helps to bring our thinking within God-given boundaries. The more I study the Word of God and try to live out the principles which I find there, the more convinced I am that true Christ-likeness begins with our thoughts. If our thinking is not right, our motives will be warped, our speech will be less than satisfactory, and our behaviour will fall short of God's standard for our lives. In order to become more like Jesus, we need to be changed by God's Spirit from the inside out – our thinking must first be brought under the authority of his Word and, once this begins to be under his control, external behaviour patterns will follow suit. Romans 12:2 is very relevant here: 'Do not conform any longer to the pattern of this world, but be transformed by the renewing of your mind. Then you will be able to test and approve what God's will is – his good, pleasing and perfect will' (emphasis mine). Would you like to have a trans-formed mind – a mind which produces right thoughts – or are you more comfortable with a mind which conforms to the unbiblical standards which you see all around you every day? 1 Corinthians 2:16 tells us that, as Christians, we have the mind of Christ. Do you stop to think about how incredibly awesome that is? Does this truth make any difference to the way you think? As we live out our Christian beliefs each day, let's show that it is indeed 'all in the mind'. Why not take Romans 12:2 as your very own verse for this week? Personalise it by praying it into your daily time with the Lord. Don't go into battle without your helmet – your mind is far too precious to be trashed by Satan.

8| The sword of the Spirit

'Take … the sword of the Spirit, which is the word of God.'
Ephesians 6:17b

This weapon is both defensive and offensive. The rest of the apostle's armour are defensive arms – girdle, breastplate, shield and helmet. But the sword both defends the Christian and wounds his enemy.
William Gurnall [1]

The sword is the final piece of armour mentioned in Ephesians 6 and, unlike all the other pieces, it is both defensive and offensive. We can use the Word of God to defend ourselves against Satan when he accuses and tempts us. Whenever we share Bible verses with a friend or use Scripture to offer praise and thanks to God, we are using his Word as an offensive weapon against the enemy. In this chapter we'll look at the importance of the sword; the relationship between the sword and the Word of God; and, finally, the relationship between the sword and the Holy Spirit.

The importance of the sword

Don't try to separate the sword from the rest of the armour. While studying the word of God is good, it is also good to let the word of God study us. The word is a window that reveals God and His world to us. But it is also a mirror that shows us as we really are. We should examine our armour in the mirror of the word and ask ourselves, 'Am I really living as I should?' As Christian soldiers, we are carrying the sword of the Spirit. But if the Holy Spirit is grieved because of our lack of integrity or our unwillingness to witness or our doubt, unbelief or discouragement, how can the sword of the Spirit be effective in our life?
Warren W Wiersbe [2]

I don't know what image you have in your mind when you try to visualise the Roman soldier's sword. It was quite a surprise for me to learn that it was a short sword, similar to a dagger. In the last chapter we saw how the enemy would fire flaming arrows at the Romans in order to 'pick off' as many of them as possible before moving in to more personal combat. The shortness of the soldier's sword meant that he had a close encounter with his enemy, using the point of his sword to stab him, with the intention of fatally wounding him. It is this picture which is relevant in our current study of the Christian's spiritual warfare. The sword of the Spirit is used when Satan comes very close to us and, because it is the Word of God, it is a very powerful weapon in our hands.

Q Why do you think that the sword is an essential weapon in the Christian's armoury?

Q Since the sword can be used for both defence and attack, what does this tell you about its relative importance in comparison with the other pieces of armour?

The sword and the Word of God

The word of God is not simply a collection of words from God, a vehicle for communicating ideas; it is living, life-changing, and dynamic as it works in us. With the incisiveness of a surgeon's knife, God's word reveals who we are and what we are not. It penetrates the core of our moral and spiritual life. It discerns what is within us, both good and evil. The demands of God's word require decisions. We must not only listen to the word; we must also let it shape our life.
Life Application Study Bible 3

The sword referred to in Ephesians 6:17 is the Word of God. Before we attempt to wield the sword of the Word of God against Satan and his army, we need to use that sword on ourselves.

Read Hebrews 4:12

Q In what way(s) does it judge 'the thoughts and attitudes of the heart'?

Are you prepared to allow God's Word, which is sharper than a two-edged sword, to cut deep into your inner self, exposing your thoughts and attitudes for what they really are? Take time now to come to the Lord and ask him to expose areas of your life which need to be brought into line with his teaching. You may wish to use the words of Psalm 139:23,24 to help you.

When considering the importance of using Bible verses against Satan, we can do no better than to look at the Lord's own example. Read the account of Jesus' temptation in the desert in Matthew 4:1–11 or in Luke 4:1–13.

Q In what way(s) did he use the sword of the Word of God to respond to Satan?

Q How can this be an encouragement to you?

Q Why was the Lord able to respond in the way he did? Psalm 119:11 might be helpful in giving your answer.

In what practical ways can you use the Word of God to put Satan to flight? You might find some of the following suggestions helpful.

Memorise some of the promises of God to recite on different occasions:

When you are afraid – Psalm 56:3,4

When Satan fires darts of accusation at you – Isaiah 54:17

When tempted to doubt your salvation – John 6:37

When you are anxious and your peace is under threat – Philippians 4:6,7

When tempted to think wrong thoughts – Philippians 4:8

When intimidated by Satan's power – 1 John 4:4.

Choose to believe that the verses which you have memorised are relevant to your particular circumstances. Reciting them is not some sort of magical formula which will get rid of difficulties immediately – you will probably have to go back to your verse more than once as, with the Lord's help, you apply it to your own situation.

Read the Bible more widely – don't restrict yourself only to the New Testament, for example, or to the gospels. Many of the psalms are relevant to contemporary life, and the book of Proverbs has 31 chapters – one for each day of the month. There are several Bible reading plans available, some of which show you how to read through the whole Bible in a year. Others take a slower pace and you can cover the entire Bible in two or three years. Ask at your Christian bookshop for details. Whether you read a lot or a little, the important thing is to get a balanced diet of biblical truth: you might want to read a New Testament passage in the morning and an Old Testament passage in the evening for instance.

The sword is provided for us; we have an open Bible. But we must know it … We must give time to it, we must get down to the depths in it, we must read the whole of the Bible, and be really steeped in the knowledge of its every part. Then at any given moment we shall have the appropriate answer, and the enemy will not only be repelled, he will be discomfited, and he will flee from us.
D Martyn Lloyd-Jones[4]

The sword and the Spirit

The relationship between the Holy Spirit and the word of God is an important one. Some tend to put the emphasis on one side or the other. But the moment we separate the Spirit and the word, we are in trouble. The late Donald Gee once said: 'All Spirit and no word, you blow up. All word and no Spirit, you dry up. Word and Spirit – you grow up.' Without the Spirit, the word is a dead letter; with the Spirit, it is a living and powerful force. The devil has a policy of 'divide and conquer', and if he can get us to separate the word from the Spirit, then he has us just where he wants us.
Selwyn Hughes 5

Ephesians 6:17 tells us that the sword belongs to the Spirit. He is the author of the Word of God and he inspired people to write that Word.

Read 2 Timothy 3:16; 2 Peter 1:21

Q Try to describe the closeness of the relationship between the Spirit and the Word of God.

Only when the sword (the Word of God) is wielded in the power of the Holy Spirit is it being used correctly. Merely quoting Scripture is insufficient – anyone can recite Bible verses, including Satan (see Matthew 4:6). Without the Holy Spirit, the sword loses much of its power. Look at the quote above from Selwyn Hughes – to what extent do you agree with what he says?

Read Hebrews 4:12

Q This description of the Word of God being 'living and active' suggests that the inspired Word of God is not just something inanimate which we use whenever it suits us. It has life, imparted by its author, the Holy Spirit. Ephesians 5:18 instructs us to 'be filled with the Spirit'. What do you suppose this means?

Q How does being filled with the Spirit help us to wield the sword of the Spirit?

> *... it is the Holy Spirit in us that uses the sword against the enemy. And the Holy Spirit has freedom to work in us only as He fills and controls us. So that one necessary prerequisite for success in waging the spiritual warfare is to have put our lives at the entire disposal, and into the entire control, of the Spirit of God ... This is the point. You cannot wield the sword of the Spirit which is the word of God unless in fact you are filled with the Spirit.*
> James Philip 6

All Christians have the Holy Spirit living in them, but to what extent are you filled with the Spirit? How much of your life is filled with his authority and control? Are there areas in your life which you don't want him to reach – areas which you are ashamed of or which you want to keep just for yourself? Take time now to begin to submit to his influence in every area of your life. The more he fills you, the more empowered you will become in your spiritual warfare.

Personal comment

One of the most important things I learned in preparing this chapter is that the sword of the Spirit is not a solitary weapon: we can't afford to separate it from the rest of the armour. In our eagerness to use the Word of God in our spiritual warfare, we must remind ourselves of the order of the pieces of armour in Ephesians 6 – it is only after we are covered with the belt of truth, the breastplate of righteousness, the shoes of peace, the shield of faith and the helmet of salvation that we are instructed to take 'the sword of the Spirit, which is the word of God'. Our use of the Word of God will only be effective in as much as our lives are consistent with the other parts of the armour. Are you a person of integrity? Are you living in a right way? Do you have a balanced grip on the truths of the gospel? Do you exercise the faith that can extinguish all the devil's flaming arrows? Is your day-to-day thinking consistent with the message of salvation which you have believed? Without these pieces of armour, we are exposed and vulnerable and easy targets for Satan and his forces.

We've also seen that the sword must never be separated from the Holy Spirit. Some years ago, when I lived in Wales, one of the women in my church often prayed for the coming Sunday services by asking that the Holy Spirit would 'work with the Word'. She realised the importance of not separating the two – she knew that, if the Spirit's power was not present when God's Word was being read and taught, then that Word would be lifeless. What an encouragement it is to remind ourselves that the Word of God, when seen as the sword of the Spirit, has an inherent power all its own!

Finally, it seems to me that the sword should never be separated from prayer. This is clearly illustrated in Exodus 17:8–13 when the Israelites defended themselves from the attack of the Amalekites – a fierce, hostile nation who delighted in killing for booty. While Moses lifted up his cane, the Israelite army were on the winning side. This is a picture of prayer (and we often need prayer support – see verse 12). Note in verse 13 that 'Joshua overcame the Amalekite army with the sword.' Prayer and God's Word go together – the raised cane of Moses needed the sharp sword of Joshua (and vice versa) in order for victory to be won.

Pray on your armour every day and take 'the sword of the Spirit, which is the word of God'.

9| Prayer – the three alls

'And pray in the Spirit on all occasions with all kinds of prayers and requests. With this in mind, be alert and always keep on praying for all the saints.'
Ephesians 6:18

Prayer is conversing, communicating with God. When we pray we talk to God, aloud or within our thoughts ... The more we pray, the more we think to pray, and as we see the results of prayer – the responses of our Father to our requests – our confidence in God's power spills over into other areas of our life.
Dallas Willard 1

I don't think that the armour of God passage ends at verse 17 of Ephesians chapter 6. Paul has now listed the six pieces of armour, but none of them would be effective in our spiritual battle if we neglected verse 18. In the same way as the soldier needs to be 'tuned in' to his commanding officer's instructions throughout the battle, so the Christian needs to maintain an open communication channel with the Lord. In this chapter, let's look at three aspects of prayer which this verse seems to highlight. We can call them 'the three alls': all occasions; all kinds of prayers and requests; and all the saints (Christian believers).

So what does it mean to pray in the Spirit? In essence, it is praying with the Holy Spirit guiding and empowering your prayer life. It is allowing Him to prompt you in whether to pray for a request at all. And if so, it is permitting Him to show you how to pray for a person or a situation, rather than assuming you know already ... All true prayer is initiated by the Spirit of God, led and guided by Him, and empowered by Him in accordance with His word. Whether your

praying takes ten minutes or ten years, He will be there every minute to lead you. Praying in the Spirit will never contradict the word of God, for the Spirit is the One who inspired the writers of Scripture in the first place.
Rich Miller 2

All occasions

'Prayer without ceasing' ... is simply walking with Jesus. As long as you're walking closely in fellowship, though there may not be words or even thoughts directed to one another, there's a sense of His presence, a communication. Sometimes you're on your knees, sometimes you're talking in the car. Sometimes you're simply rejoicing before Him as you gaze on a flower bed, quietly praising Him. It's only when you step out of fellowship by disobedience or defiance that the communication is broken. Otherwise the prayer never ends.
Mark R Littleton3

In his letters to various communities about prayer, Paul makes frequent use of such terms as 'always', 'constantly', 'unceasing', 'night and day'.

Read Romans 1:9,10; 1 Thessalonians 5:17; 2 Timothy 1:3

Q Write down what each reference says about the nature of ongoing prayer.

These verses certainly encourage us to 'pray on all occasions'. This was a practical reality for Jesus throughout his public ministry – if he prayed on all occasions, how much more is this necessary for his followers! Look up the references which follow and give examples of occasions when the Lord prayed. In some cases you might wish to read the verses that come before and after the references in order to appreciate the context of Jesus' prayers.

Verses	Times when Jesus prayed
Matthew 14:23	
Mark 1:35	
Mark 6:41	
Luke 22:44	
John 11:41,42	
John 17:6–9, 15,20,21	

Q Why is it important that we pray on all occasions and not just in time of need?

Q Are there areas mentioned above from the prayer life of the Lord which are not mirrored in your own life?

Q If so, as his follower, will you begin to include these areas in your prayer life? As you engage in battle, with the whole armour of God in place, it is so necessary to pray on all occasions in the power of the Holy Spirit.

All kinds of prayers and requests

Have you ever considered how many different kinds of prayers there are? There is silent prayer and audible prayer, prayer without ceasing and prayer that terminates, public prayer and private prayer, short prayer and extended prayer, fasting prayer and feasting prayer, prayer with one's life and prayer with one's words, rejoicing prayer and broken prayer, thanksgiving prayer and asking prayer, doctrinal prayer and emotional prayer, resisting-the-enemy prayer and standing-with-the-Lord prayer. There are probably other kinds of prayers we could consider, but the truth is that all kinds of prayers are a part of our warfare.
Mark I Bubeck [4]

In addition to praying on all occasions, God encourages us to come to him with 'all kinds of prayers and requests'. There are many different kinds of prayers in the Bible – we should never feel we are limited to using only one particular type. In our spiritual warfare we are bombarded with all kinds of attacks from our enemy, so we need to offer to our Lord all kinds of prayers and requests.

'All kinds of prayers and requests' can include the following:

Scripture prayers – this kind of prayer involves using Bible verses to pray to the Lord about a specific area of need in our lives. Read the following references and turn them into personal prayers which you can use on a regular basis. I have completed the first one as an example.

> Philippians 4:6: 'Lord, in obedience to what your word says, help me today not to be anxious about anything, but to pray to you about everything which is causing me concern. As I bring these matters to you, please help me to thank you for all you have done and are doing.'
>
> Psalm 19:14
>
> Matthew 6:33,34
>
> Romans 12:1,2

Prayers of praise and thanksgiving – these are simply expressions of love and thanksgiving to God, either in your own words or perhaps in the words of a hymn or spiritual song. Alternatively, try using ready-made prayers from his Word. Read the following verses and choose one which particularly appeals to you. Share with your group the reason for your choice.

   Psalm 28:6,7

   Psalm 144:1,2

   Ephesians 1:3

   1 Peter 1:3–5

Prayers of confession – let's not pretend that we receive no wounds while engaged in battle with the enemy. But given that the Lord has provided armour for our protection in the battle, when we sustain spiritual injury we have only ourselves to blame. We are wounded when we fail to wear pieces of the armour God has provided in the way we should. Perhaps we ignore our helmet of salvation and Satan is then able to attack our minds, and we end up thinking wrong thoughts which need to be confessed to the Lord. Or maybe we haven't always held up the shield of faith and as a result we've been pierced by the flaming arrow of paralysing fear and doubted the Lord's faithfulness. The Bible gives us lots of encouragement about confessing our sins. Read the references below and, in your own words, write down what each is saying.

   Psalm 32:5

   Psalm 51:1–4

   1 John 1:9

In what way(s) can confession enable us to 'stand our ground' in the battle?

Requests – sometimes people think that prayer is nothing more than a 'shopping list' of requests. Ephesians 6:18, by separating 'prayer' from 'requests', dispels this idea. Nevertheless, we are instructed to make requests to the Lord (see Philippians 4:6 and 1 Timothy 2:1). If the Lord knows what we need and what our desires are, why do we still need to come to him in prayer with our requests?

All the saints

Once more, we are called to be fellow-labourers together with God in prayer, as in all other ministries. The exalted Saviour ever lives to make intercession. To His redeemed people He says, 'Stay here and keep watch with me' (Matthew 26:38). There is a great work to be done in the hearts of men and there is a fierce battle to be waged with spiritual wickedness in heavenly places. Demons are to be cast out, the potencies of hell to be restrained, and the works of the devil to be destroyed. In these things it is by prayer above all other means that we shall be able to co-operate with the Captain of the Lord's host.
David M'Intyre [5]

The word 'saints' refers to Christian believers. We are to 'be alert and always keep on praying for all the saints'.

Q 'Be alert...' Why do you think this command was given? You might find 1 Peter 5:8,9 helpful in your response.

Q '...and always keep on praying'. This conveys the idea of persistence in prayer and is in the context of praying for other believers. Why should we persevere in faith and in prayer?

Q '...for all the saints'. This brings us to consider the kind of prayer known as intercession. Traditionally, to intercede meant 'to mediate or plead another's case for justice or mercy'.[6] In the Old Testament the high priest would intercede before God on behalf of the Jewish people. In John 17 we read Jesus' high-priestly prayer in which he intercedes for his disciples and all believers everywhere who would believe as a result of their message. How wide is the circle of those for whom you intercede?

Read Romans 8:26,27; Hebrews 7:24,25

Q Record who, in each case, is interceding *now* for believers.

Q How does this encourage you to pray for other Christians?

Several of Paul's letters contain examples of his intercession on behalf of Christians living in different parts of the world,

Read Ephesians 3:16–19; Philippians 1:9–11; Colossians 1:9; Philemon vs 4–6

Q From this selection, choose one to use this week as part of your intercessory praying for a Christian known to you. Personalise your prayer by inserting the person's name into the prayer.

Personal comment

In this chapter, we've touched on only a fraction of all that could have been included about prayer in a Christian's life. I've certainly been challenged to consider what could possibly be meant by praying on all occasions, with all kinds of prayers, for all Christians. I think most of us feel we're doing quite well if we pray on some occasions, with some kind of prayer, for some Christians! Isn't it so good to know that we can have the Holy Spirit's help in praying in any situation and at any time? I remember seeing a notice on the office door of a school chaplain which said that he was available for consultation only between certain hours. How different is the Lord who encourages us to pray to him 'on all occasions'! How well are you doing in the realm of praying with 'all kinds of prayers and requests'? An important kind of prayer, particularly effective in our spiritual warfare, is doctrinal prayer – prayer that draws on the truths of the Bible which remind Christians of the resources available to them as a result of Jesus' finished work on the cross. For more help with this kind of praying, I would recommend Mark Bubeck's booklet, Spiritual Warfare Prayers.[7] And what about persisting in prayer for all Christians everywhere? Do you have a group of Christians whom you pray for regularly? This is good, but can I challenge you to widen the circle, little by little? I read of someone who mentally divided the world into seven parts and allocated one part to each day of the week to commit to pray for Christians unknown to her but known to God. By doing this, she was able to go some way to 'praying for all the saints'.

Or what about on a more local level – in your own town or city? Do you pray for Christians in other churches? Do you long to see the Lord using believers across denominations so that he is glorified in the salvation of unbelievers and the strengthening of bonds of commitment between his followers? We might be individual soldiers but we are not fighting a personal battle – we are part of a large army whom God has equipped to stand for him against the forces of evil. Let's commit to pray regularly for other Christians who fight with us against the same enemy, remembering the words of 2 Chronicles 20:15: 'Do not be afraid or discouraged because of this vast army. For the battle is not yours, but God's.' As a result of Jesus' death on the cross, we can be confident that God has already won the victory for us and it is our task to hold on to that and to the inheritance which is already ours. 'With this in mind, be alert and always keep on praying for all the saints.'

10| **Concluding questions**

'I have fought the good fight, I have finished the race, I have kept the faith. Now there is in store for me the crown of righteousness, which the Lord, the righteous Judge, will award to me on that day – and not only to me, but also to all who have longed for his appearing.'
2 Timothy 4:7,8

Viewed from the short perspective, there will be times when it seems that our enemy has won the day. Such limited sight does not tell the whole story, however. Paul's years of imprisonment at Caesarea and Rome must have seemed to the short-sighted to be a triumph for the enemy. Yet, during those years some of God's greatest victories over darkness were won. Paul's letters to the Ephesians, Philippians, and Colossians were all written from prison. He wrote Ephesians 6:10–18's message of victory, which has been shared through the centuries and around the world. Hold on to the vision of yourself as nothing but a winner.
Mark I Bubeck [1]

As we come to the final chapter of this study on the armour of God, it might be a good idea to read through the whole of Ephesians 6:10–18 as a complete unit. Below is this passage taken from JB Phillips' *New Testament in Modern English*.

'In conclusion be strong – not in yourselves but in the Lord, in the power of His boundless resource. Put on God's complete armour so that you can successfully resist all the devil's methods of attack. For our fight is not against any physical enemy: it is against organizations and powers that are spiritual. We are up against the unseen power that controls this dark world, and spiritual agents from the very headquarters of evil. Therefore you must wear the whole armour of God that you may be able to resist evil in its day of power, and that even when you have fought to a standstill you may still stand your ground. Take your stand then with truth as your belt, righteousness your breast-plate, the gospel of peace firmly on your feet, salvation as your helmet and in your hand the sword of the Spirit, the word of God. Above all be sure you take faith as your shield, for it can quench every burning missile the enemy hurls at you. Pray at all times with every kind of spiritual prayer, keeping alert and persistent as you pray for all Christ's men and women.' 2

The content of this Bible passage should by now be very familiar to you, but what *practical* difference has it made in your life? If we read and study God's Word and it has no life-changing effect upon us, we are like the person mentioned in James 1:22–24 who takes no action to adjust his appearance after having looked in the mirror as he immediately forgets what he has just seen. How much better for us to be like the person in verse 25 – are you *doing* what you have learned about in this study? Let's use this chapter to revise what we've been learning over the last few weeks and to challenge ourselves to *do* what God's Word says.

Are you a James 1:25 person?

If we heard a sermon every day of the week, and an angel from heaven were the preacher, yet, if we rested in hearing only, it would never bring us to heaven. Mere hearers are self-deceivers; and self-deceit will be found the worst deceit at last ... It is not talking, but walking, that will bring us to heaven.
Matthew Henry 3

James 1:25 makes it clear that it is only when we *live* the Bible that we can fully appreciate its blessings. From each of the chapters in this study, select the main principle (or principles) learned and how you are putting these into practice in your spiritual battle with the enemy.

Chapter	Principle learned	How to put into practice
1		
2		
3		
4		
5		
6		
7		
8		
9		

What are you wearing today?

Stand up, stand up for Jesus!
Stand in His strength alone:
The arm of flesh will fail you;
Ye dare not trust your own.
Put on the gospel armour,
Each piece put on with prayer;
Where duty calls, or danger,
Be never wanting there.
George Duffield 4

I'm going to share with you a dream which I've often had. I dream that I've gone out of the house wearing the wrong clothes! I find myself on the way to an important speaking engagement wearing my old shabby work-clothes which I wear when decorating! Each time, in my dream, I ask myself: 'Why have I come out again not properly dressed? I hate being like this – why do I do it?' Well, hopefully, I'll never find myself in this situation in reality and I'm sure the same is true for you too. We make it an essential part of our daily routine to put on the right clothes in the morning before we go out. But are you aware that, the minute you wake up to start a new day, you are about to enter into conflict with the enemy and need to put on, not just your ordinary clothes, but the appropriate battle gear? Would you dare leave home not properly dressed as far as this is concerned? If we are to fight, then we must be dressed for the fight. Read the questions below, answering them as fully as possible.

Q How do you think this armour should be put on?

Q How often do you think this armour should be put on?

Q Once the armour is on, is it visible to other people?

Q How do I know when a piece is missing?

Q How important is it to 'pray on' each piece of the armour at the start of the day?

If you haven't yet begun to do so, you might wish to start praying each piece of armour into position on a daily basis. Think carefully about the purpose of each piece, using the material in this study if that would be helpful, and prayerfully put it on. For example, I might pray regarding the belt of truth:

'Lord, I thank you that your word is truth, that it is completely right and dependable in all circumstances. Help me today to recognise Satan's lies and to instantly reject them. Please help me to be a person of integrity in each situation that I'll be involved in today. Help me to be truthful in all my relationships with the people I meet.'

Of course, I wouldn't learn this off by heart and merely repeat it word for word each day, but these are the lines along which I might pray. You might find it helpful to write out sample prayers for each piece of the armour and use these *as a guide* for praying the armour into place.

Who is my armour?

To be strong in the Lord, we are told to put on the whole armour of God. Paul wrote to the Romans, 'Therefore let us cast off the works of darkness, and let us put on the armour of light' (13:12 NKJV). The armour of light is sturdy kingdom clothing that not only protects us, but also exemplifies Christlike character.
Cynthia Heald [5]

I'm sure that you're now able to name all the pieces that make up the armour of God. The armour can be worn only by the Christian believer – we know this because we are told to whom Paul wrote the initial letter, ie the believers in the church at Ephesus. In addition, truth, righteousness, peace, salvation, faith and God's Word have real meaning only when seen in the context of Christian experience. We can go even further – each piece of armour can be directly linked to the life and character of the Lord Jesus Christ. In fact, he is our armour! In Romans 13:14 we read: 'clothe yourselves with the Lord Jesus Christ'. Various Bible verses clearly indicate that Jesus is the Christian's armour.

Read Psalm 27:1; John 1:1; John 14:6; 1 Corinthians 1:30; Ephesians 2:14; Hebrews 12:2

Q Show how these verses relate to the relevant pieces of armour which we've been studying.

Q What encouragement do you get from knowing that Jesus is your armour?

Q How does this help you to stand firm against the enemy?

Read John 8:12; Romans 13:12

Q In John 8:12 we read that Jesus said: 'I am the light of the world' and in Romans 13:12 Paul urges us to 'put aside the deeds of darkness and put on the armour of light'. From your reading of these two verses, what does this further tell you about the relationship between the Lord and the believer's armour?

As we conclude this study on being dressed for success by living under the protection of God's armour, I urge you to:

◆ Reaffirm the wonderful position that you have as a believer in the Lord Jesus

◆ Realise once again that you are not fighting the enemy alone – the battle belongs to the Lord

◆ Remember the victory has already been won through the death and resurrection of Jesus – therefore, Satan is a defeated foe and has no authority over you

◆ Remind yourself that the Lord has given you all the resources you need to live a victorious Christian life – you are his child, you have his Spirit living within you, you have his armour round about you, and you have the great privilege of being able to enter into his presence at any time through prayer.

Doubt your own strength, but never doubt Christ's ... Christian, take special care not to trust in the armour of God, but in the God of the armour. All your weapons are only 'mighty through God' (2 Corinthians 10:4).
William Gurnall 6

Personal comment

I've learned so much from studying Ephesians 6:10–18. I hope that you have too. I don't want our learning to be an end in itself, but to be a means by which we are motivated to put into practice the principles which we have come across through reading the Bible references. This passage of scripture is full of action words – be strong; put on; take your stand; stand firm; take up; be alert; keep on praying. In the same way as a soldier must carry out his military responsibilities in unwavering obedience to his commander, we too, as Christians, need to obey the instructions given to us in Ephesians 6:10–18. Ongoing obedience to the Lord's commands is essential for spiritual victory. Let's make sure that we don't allow Satan to deceive us into thinking that, having completed a Bible study on the armour of God, we now don't need to do anything more. Refer to the Bible references, questions and answers in this study again and again if it will help you in your battle with the enemy. As you continue for the rest of your earthly life to engage in spiritual warfare with the devil and his army, remember James 4:7 – 'Submit yourselves, then, to God. Resist the devil, and he will flee from you.'

| Endnotes

Chapter 1

1 Rich Miller, *The Armor of God* (Part 1), Freedom in Christ Ministries. www.ficm.org/ArmorArchive.html

2 Warren W Wiersbe, *What to Wear to the War*, Back to the Bible, 1997, p8.

3 D Martyn Lloyd Jones, *The Christian Soldier*, The Banner of Truth Trust, 1977, p27.

4 G Campbell Morgan, 'The Opposing Forces of the Religious Life – The Devil' in *The Westminster Pulpit*, vol 3, Pickering and Inglis.

5 James Philip, *Christian Warfare and Armour*, Christian Focus Publications Ltd, 1989, p7.

6 Jerry Bridges, 'Engaging The Unseen Foe', *Discipleship Journal*, no. 19 (Jan/Feb 1984). (Text taken from CD-ROM, published by NavPress. Visit www.navpress.com/dj.asp for details.)

Chapter 2

1 Bill Bussard, 'Do You Hear The Roaring Lion?' *Discipleship Journal*, no. 2 (Mar/Apr 1981) (Text taken from CD-ROM, published by NavPress. Visit www.navpress.com/dj.asp for details.)

2 Timothy Warner, 'Satan Hates You And Has A Terrible Plan For Your Life', *Discipleship Journal*, no. 81 (May/June 1994). (Text taken from CD Rom, published by NavPress. Visit www.discipleshipjournal.org for details.)

3 Frederick S Leahy, *Satan Cast Out*, The Banner of Truth Trust, 1975, p47.

4 Eugene H Peterson, *The Message*, NavPress, 1993, p483.

5 Mark I Bubeck, *Overcoming the Adversary*, Moody Press, 1984, p26.

6 Neil T Anderson, *Winning Spiritual Warfare*, Harvest House Publishers, 1991, p8. Used with permission.

Chapter 3

1 Mary Whelchel, *What Would Jesus Think?* Chariot Victor, 1998, p44.

2 James Philip, *Christian Warfare and Armour*, Christian Focus, 1989, p16.

3 Cynthia Heald, *When the Father Holds You Close*, Thomas Nelson, 1999, p122.

4 Matthew Henry, *Concise Commentary on the Whole Bible*, Moody Press, 1983, p914.

5 Bill Hybels, *Actions Speak Louder Than Words*, Marshall Pickering, 1998, p63.

6 Jerry White, 'The Power of Integrity' in *Discipleship Journal*, no. 104 (Mar/Apr 1998), p34.

Chapter 4

1 Mary Whelchel, *Prepared to Fight, The Christian Working Woman* – A Nationwide Radio Ministry, 1993. (This organisation broadcasts in the USA and elsewhere. See www.christianworkingwoman.org)

2 Cheryl Sneeringer, *Bible Lectures on Ephesians*, CBS Austin North. http://home.austin.rr.com/sneeringer/cheryl/ephesians12/

3 T Croskery in *The Pulpit Commentary*, ed H D M Spence and Joseph S Exell, Hendrickson, vol 20, pp268–69.

4 Jan Silvious, *The Five-Minute Devotional – Meditations for the Busy Woman*, Zondervan, 1991, p30.

5 Warren and Ruth Myers, 'Weapons That Work', *Discipleship Journal*, no. 81 (May/June 1994) (Text taken from CD-ROM, published by NavPress. Visit www.navpress.com/dj.asp for details.)

Chapter 5

1 Charles Spurgeon, *Spiritual Warfare in a Believer's Life*, ed. Robert Hall, Emerald Books, 1993, p146. Used with permission.

2 William Gurnall, *The Christian in Complete Armour*, vol 2, The Banner of Truth Trust, 1988, pp356,357.

3 Warren W Wiersbe, *What To Wear To The War*, Back to the Bible, 1997, pp48,49.

4 Warren W Wiersbe, *What To Wear To The War*, Back to the Bible, 1997, p53.

5 Rich Miller, *The Armor of God (Part 9)*, Freedom in Christ Ministries. www.ficm.org/ArmorArchive.html

Chapter 6

1 Selwyn Hughes, *Every Day with Jesus – the Armour of God*, CWR, 1993, week four, day seven.

2 Jan Silvious, *The 5-Minute Devotional – Meditations for the Busy Woman*, Zondervan, 1991, p162.

3 Mary Whelchel, 'Satan's Flaming Arrows', *The Christian Working Woman*, Friday 10 December 1999. (This organisation broadcasts in the USA and elsewhere. See www.christianworkingwoman.org)

4 Clinton E Arnold, 'Where Do We Draw The Line?' *Discipleship Journal*, no. 101 (Sep/Oct 1997). (Text taken from CD-ROM, published by NavPress. Visit www.navpress.com/dj.aspg for details.)

5 Carol Kent, *Tame Your Fears*, NavPress, 1993.

Chapter 7

1 James Philip, *Christian Warfare and Armour*, Christian Focus, 1989, p71.

2 Charles Spurgeon, *Spiritual Warfare in a Believer's Life*, Emerald Books, 1993, p132.

3 Cheryl Sneeringer, *Bible Lectures on Ephesians*, CBS Austin North. http://home.austin.rr.com/sneeringer/cheryl/ephesians12/

4 Mary Whelchel, *Prepared to Fight*, booklet prepared by The Christian Working Woman, 1993, p16.

5 Mary Whelchel, *What Would Jesus Think?* Chariot Victor, 1998, p144.

Chapter 8

1 William Gurnall, *The Christian in Complete Armour*, vol 3, The Banner of Truth Trust, 1996, pp222,223.

2 Warren W Wiersbe, *What To Wear To The War*, Back to the Bible, 1997, pp82,83.

3 *Life Application Study Bible: New Living Translation*, Tyndale House, 1996, p1964.

4 D Martyn Lloyd-Jones, *The Christian Soldier*, The Banner of Truth Trust, 1977, p335.

5 Selwyn Hughes, *Every Day with Jesus – the Armour of God*, CWR, 1993, week six, day four.

6 James Philip, *Christian Warfare and Armour*, Christian Focus, 1989, p86.

Chapter 9

1 Dallas Willard, *The Spirit of the Disciplines*, Hodder & Stoughton, 1996, pp191,192.

2 Rich Miller, 'The Armor of God' (Part 15) Freedom in Christ Ministries. www.ficm.org/ArmorArchive.html

3 Mark R Littleton, 'Prayer Unceasing?', *Discipleship Journal*, no. 26 (Mar/Apr 1985). (Text taken from CD-ROM, published by NavPress. Visit www.nav-press.com/dj.asp for details.)

4 Mark I Bubeck, *Overcoming the Adversary*, Moody Press, 1984, pp122,123.

5 David M'Intyre, *The Hidden Life of Prayer*, Bethany House, 1993, pp86,87.

6 *Life Application Study Bible: New Living Translation*, Tyndale House, 1996, p2200.

7 Mark I Bubeck, *Spiritual Warfare Prayers*, Moody Press, 1997.

Chapter 10

1 Mark I Bubeck, *Overcoming the Adversary*, Moody Press, 1984, p139.

2 J B Phillips, *New Testament in Modern English* (revised edition), Harper Collins, 1972, p335.

3 Matthew Henry, *Concise Commentary on the Whole Bible*, Moody Press, 1983, p970.

4 George Duffield, 'Stand up, stand up for Jesus', third verse, in Christian Hymns, Evangelical Movement of Wales, 1977, p717.

5 Cynthia Heald, *When The Father Holds You Close*, Thomas Nelson, 1999, p121.

6 William Gurnall, *The Christian in Complete Armour, volume 1*, Banner of Truth Trust, 1988, pp65–67.

Other Resources from Scripture Union

Bodybuilders

Small group resource

A highly relational small group resource that's flexible and fun to use. Six outlines in each book contain notes for leaders, prayer and worship ideas, photocopiable sheets of interactive and in-depth Bible study material and ideas for personal study during the week.

A Fresh Encounter (David Bolster) 1 85999 586 1

Designed for Great Things (Anton Bauhmohl) 1 85999 585 3

Living for the King ('Tricia Williams) 1 85999 584 5

Relationship Building (Lance Pierson) 1 85999 582 9

Surviving Under Pressure (Christopher Griffiths & Stephen Hathway) 1 85999 587 X

Growing Through Change (Lance Pierson) 1 85999 583 7

210x140mm pb 32pp   £3.50

Understanding the Bible

John Stott

A format pb 192pp £2.99

ISBN 1 85999 225 0

A special budget edition of a widely-acclaimed classic bestseller. Outstanding Christian teacher and author John Stott examines the cultural, social, geographical and historical background of the Bible, outlining the story and explaining the message.

Understanding the Bible

John Stott

245x160mm hb 170pp £9.99

1 85999 569 1

A brand new edition in full colour. Revised and updated text is illustrated with charts, diagrams and wonderful colour photos. An ideal gift!

Christian Life and Today's World package

(Video editor: Rob Purbrick)

ISBN 1 85999 576 4

How can we take up the challenge of living as Christians in a post-modern society? From SU and LBC comes another stimulating small group resource containing video, accompanying workbook for group leaders and book of articles written by members of the LBC faculty.

A format pb 192pp + workbook 60pp + video £25.00

Light from a Dark Star

Where's God when my world falls apart?

Wayne Kirkland

ISBN: 1 85999 515 2, £4.99

It's the big question that won't go away. Why does God allow suffering? There are no simple answers in this book. No attempts to shrug off the serious challenges to faith which the question raises. Rather it engages compassionately with the sufferings of real people, grappling with slippery issues, in a discovery of some intriguing perspectives.

Knowing God's Ways

A user's guide to the Old Testament

Patton Taylor

ISBN: 1 85999 349 4, £6.99

Do you find the Old Testament difficult to get into? If you've been looking for some help in making sense of it all, then this book by a professor at Union Theological College in Belfast is what you've been looking for! His accessible. user-friendly approach will help you gain a clear overview of the Old Testament, understand different genres, and apply biblical teaching to today's world.

Journey into the Bible

John Drane

ISBN: 1 85999 409 1, £4.99

In his usual thought-provoking and accessible style John Drane gives a stimulating introduction to many of the issues raised by reading the Bible today. Designed especially for those who are struggling to come to terms with the Bible.

Dangerous Praying

Inspirational Ideas for individuals and groups

David Spriggs

ISBN: 1 85999335 4, £6.99

Drawing on Paul's letter to the Ephesians, this creative book challenges us to be bold when we pray, both in what we pray for and how we pray. David Spriggs presents us with 101 practical ideas and strategies to help us develop a courageous prayer life, whether in a group or individually.

Ready to Grow

Practical steps to knowing God better

Alan Harkness

ISBN 0 949720 71 2, £5.99

An attractive and practical book to encourage believers to make time with God a regular part of their lives. Includes chapters on preparation, getting started, the practicalities, sharing what you have learned, and different methods of combining Bible reading and prayer.

Faith and Common Sense

Living boldly, choosing wisely

David Dewey

ISBN: 1 85999 302 8, £4.99

This unusual book explores how we can live riskily yet sensibly. Drawing on the lives of key Bible characters like Peter, the author first lays a solid biblical and theological foundation for achieving a balance. Then follows a practical look at areas in our lives where a need for that balance is vital - healing, the gifts of the Spirit, work, money, failure and guidance.

The Bible Unwrapped

Developing your Bible skills

David Dewey

ISBN: 1 85999 533 0, £5.99

Is the Bible something of a closed book to you? Here you'll find help in finding your way around the Bible, and in grasping the big picture of the Bible's message. You'll also learn to appreciate the different types of literature in the Bible and be introduced to eight different approaches to Bible study. Clear and accurate charts and diagrams and a helpful glossary add value.